T0327009

I highly recommend this theologically rich yet highly accessible introduction to John's Gospel! Drawing on decades of faithful scholarship, Professor Köstenberger is a reliable guide to help readers grasp John's storyline and core message.

BRIAN J. TABB
academic dean and associate professor of biblical studies,
Bethlehem College & Seminary

Andreas Köstenberger has written another engaging work on the Gospel of John which displays his erudition, here worn with a light touch, his deep knowledge of the Fourth Gospel, and his love for Jesus Messiah whom John describes as Savior of the world. His explanation of the seven signs of Jesus is an inspiration to all Christians who seek to have an ever deeper understanding of the Word of God.

ECKHARD J. SCHNABEL
Mary French Rockefeller Distinguished Professor of
New Testament, Gordon-Conwell Theological Seminary

It was Ernst Käsemann who said that the Gospel of John is shallow enough for a baby to wade in but deep enough for an elephant to drown. Andreas Köstenberger is one who has been swimming in the deep end of the Johannine pool for a long time, and it shows in this easy-to-read guide to the theology of the Fourth Gospel, a theology of an eyewitness of Jesus himself! Students and pastors alike will gain new insights into this crucial telling of the good news by working through this little primer.

BEN WITHERINGTON III
Amos Professor of New Testament for Doctoral Studies,
Asbury Theological Seminary

In this introduction to John's Gospel, Köstenberger provides a clear, trust-worthy guide to understanding and applying the powerful message of this captivating book. He draws from decades of first-rate Johannine scholarship in offering readers an engaging, well-organized, persuasively written account. You can do no better than *Signs of the Messiah* for a reliable historical, literary and theological primer on John's Gospel. Highly recommended!

J. SCOTT DUVALL
J. C. and Mae Fuller Professor of New Testament,
Ouachita Baptist University

Signs of the Messiah is a compelling journey through the Gospel of John, and Köstenberger, with his expertise on this remarkable text of Scripture, is amply qualified to be your tour guide. The work is written in a conver-sational style, but that is not to say the book avoids subtlety and intricacy, both of which are present in abundance as the reader is led through the cycles and discourses of the Fourth Gospel. I especially appreciated the author's attention to *how* the narrative is constructed by the inspired writer. This book promises to be a substantial foundation for anyone planning to employ this Gospel in the ministry of the word.

ABRAHAM KURUVILLA
senior research professor of preaching and pastoral ministries,
Dallas Theological Seminary

It is a gift when a New Testament scholar applies years of biblical and theo-logical expertise to a resource designed for teachers and preachers in the local church. Here we find thoughtful engagement with all the major sec-tions of John, coupled with scholarly insights and practical application. With special emphasis on the signs of Jesus, Köstenberger provides an illuminat-ing and helpful resource for those desiring to teach or study this amazing story of Jesus!

ROGER SEVERINO
minister of leadership development,
Brentwood Baptist Church, Brentwood, TN

This volume offers numerous fresh insights into John's Gospel. It defends Johannine authorship, draws skillfully on scholarship and the author's own original observations, and demonstrates how the layout of the Fourth Gospel contributes to its claims and message. It highlights traditional themes like believing, mission, and the supremacy of Christ—in particular his messiahship. But it does so in innovative ways and often with an urgency that makes parts of the book into a page-turner. Pastors, teachers, students, and all others who want to understand this Gospel and pass along its good news to others will find this book to be an outstanding resource.

ROBERT W. YARBROUGH
professor of New Testament,
Covenant Theological Seminary

Forgoing unnecessary academic lingo, Köstenberger writes this work in a way that communicates well for pastors and lay readers. After a robust and, I believe, persuasive defense of the Fourth Gospel's authorship by the apostle John, Köstenberger works through the Gospel in ways both practical and edifying.

CRAIG S. KEENER
F. M. and Ada Thompson Professor of Biblical Studies,
Asbury Theological Seminary

Quite often resources on John focus upon a single aspect of the gospel whether that be its major literary features, theological themes, background, or the historical events described therein. What Köstenberger has accomplished is a volume that shows how these elements are interwoven in the very flow of the book itself. It provides a cohesive picture of how John builds his argument so that the pastor and teacher cannot merely talk about components of the book but teach expositionally through it. This work serves as a crucial primer for anyone who wants to grasp each passage within John's Gospel as John intended it.

ABNER CHOU
John F. MacArthur Endowed Fellow,
The Master's University

Signs of the Messiah is a brief and insightful primer on John's Gospel. Köstenberger is particularly attentive to the literary shaping of John, along with ways that the fourth Gospel assumes and complements the other three. Köstenberger provides his own theological reflection on John's Gospel in an ongoing conversation with the reader. An accessible and engaging book.

JEANNINE BROWN

professor of New Testament and director of online programs,
Bethel Seminary

The religious leaders and people of Jesus' day asked for evidence— "Show us a sign!"—that would prove he was who he claimed to be. And Jesus did just that through the signs described in the Gospel of John. This latest work by Dr. Andreas Köstenberger demonstrates once again he is one of the foremost experts in Johannine studies, particularly the Gospel of John. Whether you are a Bible student, teacher, or preacher of John's Gospel, you will find Dr. Köstenberger's book both scholarly and practical. This concise book is packed with information, rich in insights, and understandable for all. As a pastor and professor, I always value a book like this—and I know I will turn to this one often.

DAVID L. BURGGRAFF

professor of theological studies, Shepherds Theological Seminary;
executive pastor, Colonial Baptist Church, Cary, NC

In *Signs of the Messiah*, Dr. Andreas Köstenberger accomplishes a task that is not an easy one. He has written an introduction to the Gospel of John that demonstrates both his wide-ranging fluency with Johannine scholarship and his ability to make that scholarship accessible to a broader audience. On every page, the reader will recognize that here is an exceptional scholar who knows not only the Gospel of John and the scholarship surrounding it, but also that here is a talented communicator who can explain both the text and the scholarship with great clarity to an audience just beginning to study the fourth Gospel.

C. SCOTT SHIDEMANTLE

professor of biblical studies and Bible core coordinator,
Geneva College, Beaver Falls, PA

SIGNS
OF THE MESSIAH

SIGNS
OF THE MESSIAH

*An Introduction to
John's Gospel*

ANDREAS J. KÖSTENBERGER

LEXHAM PRESS

Signs of the Messiah: An Introduction to John's Gospel

Copyright 2021 Andreas J. Köstenberger

Lexham Press, 1313 Commercial St., Bellingham, WA 98225
LexhamPress.com

Print ISBN 9781683594550
Digital ISBN 9781683594567
Library of Congress Control Number 2020948474

Lexham Editorial: Derek R. Brown, Elizabeth Vince, Danielle Thevenaz
Cover Design: Kristen Cork
Book Design and Typesetting: Abigail Stocker

In loving memory
of the apostle John
the son of Zebedee

who, though dead, still speaks
through the witness he bore
to the Word, the Christ,
the Son of God
Jesus of Nazareth
Messiah
Lord of all
Savior of the world.
"As the Father sent me,
so I am sending you."
(John 20:21)

Contents

· Part 3 ·
CONCLUSION *to* BOOK OF SIGNS
(*John 11–12*)
and BOOK OF EXALTATION
(*John 13–21*)

List of Figures

Introduction

"GIVE ME A SIGN!"

H ave you ever asked God for a sign? If so, did he give you one? What kind of sign was it?

In Old Testament times, Gideon asked God for a sign. Later, Hezekiah did as well. Moses performed mighty "signs and wonders" during the exodus. The prophets, too, at times acted out signs, symbolic gestures conveying God's message to his people. At one time, Isaiah went about stripped down to his undergarments to convey God's impending judgment on the people of Israel. Their fate was sealed: they had rejected God, and as a result, they would be exiled to Babylon.

Jesus was asked for signs.

Matthew reports that, one time, when the Sadducees and Pharisees asked Jesus for a sign, he responded that the only sign people would receive was the "sign of Jonah" (Matt 16:4). Jonah, the Old Testament prophet, was in the belly of the big fish for three days and three nights before God delivered him. This, Jesus told those who asked him for a sign, was the only sign he would give them. In fact, God had already given that sign to them. Did they believe in the God who could deliver, the God who could save people from death and even raise the dead?

John, too, records people asking Jesus for a sign. "What sign do you show us for doing these things?" the temple authorities challenged Jesus after he had cleared the temple area of the merchants as a sign of his messianic authority (John 2:18).

After Jesus had fed a crowd of five thousand, Jesus' opponents were at it again. "Then what sign do you do, that we may see and believe you?" they asked (John 6:30–31).

"Give us a sign, and we'll believe," they insisted. Well, did he give them a sign? And did they believe?

In his Gospel, John tells us that Jesus, the Messiah, did indeed give people multiple messianic signs. And yet, they did not believe.

Theologians call this "theodicy"—the vindication of God and his righteousness.

You see, God held up his end of the bargain—Jesus performed seven startling signs (the perfect number). And yet people still would not believe.

John's point is that people's unbelief was their own fault. The problem was not that God, through Jesus, failed to provide tangible evidence that he was real. No, the problem was that people asked for signs, but when Jesus gave them a sign, they didn't like the one he gave them and kept asking for more. He fed the multitudes, he healed the sick, he even opened the eyes of a man born blind—and for an encore, he raised a dead man whose body had been in the tomb for four days.

What more evidence do you need?

Have you ever talked with someone who asked you a barrage of questions about faith and, no matter what you said, they kept asking more questions—and in the end, they walked away without any sign of commitment, without any indication that the evidence you presented made even the slightest bit of difference?

The story John tells us is all about this. It is all about the signs for which people asked Jesus—the signs he gave them, and what they did (or didn't) do with them.

In this brief introduction to John's Gospel, I have tried to keep a close eye on the big picture—the main plot line and the flow of argument. I've written this book (which originated as a series of "For the Church Workshop" lectures I gave at Midwestern Baptist Theological Seminary at the invitation of President Jason Allen) to walk you step by step through John's unfolding narrative of Jesus the Messiah and Son of God.

I recommend you read this book while you read through John's Gospel. In this way, this short book can serve as a companion that hopefully will further illumine John's core message—that Jesus is the Messiah, the Son of God—so that you might believe and have eternal, abundant life in him. This is my hope, and this is my prayer for you.

Thank you for picking up this little book. May God honor your openness and commitment to him. I know he will.

PART 1

◇ ◇ ◇

AUTHORSHIP, PROLOGUE, *and* CANA CYCLE

(JOHN 1-4)

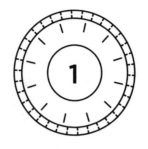

AUTHORSHIP
AND
JOHN'S
PROLOGUE

—

T hank you for joining me as we set out on a journey to explore the theology of John, especially in his Gospel. I love the Gospel of John because John is profoundly theological and has such a deep grasp of who Jesus is. However, talking about *John's* theology and his Gospel raises some important questions: Who was John? And what was his relationship with Jesus?

In this chapter, I'll first discuss the authorship of John's Gospel, and then I'll move into a discussion of John's prologue, the first eighteen verses of the Gospel. The next two chapters will be devoted to a close examination of the so-called "Cana Cycle" (John 2–4), which includes Jesus' initial sign—the turning of water into wine—as well as the temple clearing, his conversations with Nicodemus and the Samaritan woman, and the healing of the gentile centurion's son.

I believe introductory matters are vital for the study of a given book of Scripture: authorship, date, provenance, destination, occasion, and purpose.[1] These topics are not merely something you determine and then leave behind as you go on to study a passage in a given book. Rather, you need to constantly keep the author's identity in mind as you try to discern the authorial intent underlying that passage.

It's also important to use a sound hermeneutical method. In what follows, I am presupposing what I call the "hermeneutical triad"—that is, we'll be looking at the interpretation of John's Gospel through the trifocal lens of history, literature, and theology.[2] We'll try to keep in

---

1. See Andreas J. Köstenberger, L. Scott Kellum, and Charles L. Quarles, *The Cradle, the Cross, and the Crown: An Introduction to the New Testament,* 2nd ed. (Nashville: B&H Academic, 2016), for which I wrote the chapter on John's Gospel.

2. See my book, with Richard D. Patterson, *Invitation to Biblical Interpretation: Exploring the Hermeneutical Triad of History, Literature, and Theology,* 2nd ed. (Grand Rapids: Kregel, 2020).

mind any relevant historical-cultural background issues. We'll also be mindful of literary devices such as chiasm or *inclusio* and narrative features such as plot or characterization. When it comes to theology, we'll try to discern any Old Testament usage, whether by way of direct quotation, allusion, or typology, and we'll remember that John is the "spiritual Gospel." By that I meant that he focuses primarily on Christology, the true identity of the Lord Jesus Christ as Messiah and Son of God, in keeping with his purpose statement (20:30–31).

I hope to help you build a solid foundation as you study, preach, or teach John's Gospel, and by extension, other books of the Bible. I'll try to model sound exegesis and hermeneutics in breaking down the Gospel unit by unit and to discern the central message in each unit within the scope of the entire Gospel. In this way, I hope you'll be thoroughly equipped to grasp for yourself and communicate to others the amazing spiritual truths contained in John's Gospel.

WHO WROTE JOHN'S GOSPEL?

Let's first turn our attention to the question of who wrote John's Gospel. Many critical scholars today don't believe the apostle John wrote the Gospel that bears his name. Some contend that another person named John, perhaps someone commonly called "John the elder," wrote the Gospel. Others argue that a so-called "Johannine community," which traced its roots to the apostle, wrote the Gospel sometime after John's death. Yet others say someone else wrote the Gospel, such as Lazarus.

I believe this is not merely an academic squabble. It is important to determine who the author of John's Gospel is and what his relationship to Jesus is because the credibility of a given writing largely depends on the credibility of its author. If the apostle John, one of the twelve apostles—and one of only three in Jesus' inner circle—wrote the Gospel, this would make the Gospel highly authoritative, as John is one of the most important eyewitnesses of Jesus.

If, on the other hand, a community of John's followers wrote the Gospel based on some Johannine traditions after the apostle had already died, the connection would be a lot more indirect, and the Gospel would therefore be less credible and authoritative. At best, it would reflect indirect rather than direct eyewitness testimony. At worst, it would project the history of such a Johannine community onto the life and times of Jesus, as J. Louis Martyn, Raymond Brown, and others have argued.[3] So, the authority of John's Gospel hinges to a significant extent on the identity of its author.[4]

How, then, do we determine the author of John's Gospel? There are two main avenues: internal and external evidence. Sometimes people start with the external evidence—meaning they examine who Christians in the early centuries of the church identified as the author of John's Gospel. I, however, prefer to start with the internal evidence, meaning I examine clues in the text itself that identify its author. So, let's start there.

INTERNAL EVIDENCE

Formally, like all the Gospels, John's Gospel is anonymous. Unlike the New Testament letters, it doesn't start out by saying, for example, "I, the apostle John, wrote this Gospel." That's because a Gospel is not person-to-person or person-to-group communication like an epistle is. Rather, as Richard Bauckham and others have argued in *The Gospels for All Christians*, a Gospel is a universal document that sets forth the story of Jesus more broadly to a wide-reading public.[5]

---

3. See J. Louis Martyn, *History and Theology in the Fourth Gospel*, 3rd ed. (Louisville: Westminster John Knox, 2003); Raymond E. Brown, *The Community of the Beloved Disciple: The Life, Loves, and Hates of an Individual Church in New Testament Times* (Mahwah, NJ: Paulist, 1979).

4. The most recent contribution is Hugo Méndez, "Did the Johannine Community Exist?," *JSNT* 40 (2020): 350–74. While appropriately questioning the validity of the "Johannine community hypothesis" (on which see further below), the author doesn't stop there but goes on to argue that John's Gospel is a big fat lie—a forgery! Both John's Gospel and his letters are "probably fabrications"(!), "a chain of literary forgeries."

5. Richard Bauckham, ed., *The Gospels for All Christians: Rethinking the Gospel Audiences* (Grand Rapids: Eerdmans, 1997).

The "Disciple Whom Jesus Loved"

While the Gospel of John does not explicitly identify its author, when we investigate it for clues regarding its authorship, we find several important internal pieces of information. To begin with, we notice several references to a person called "the disciple whom Jesus loved." He is first mentioned in the account of the upper room, where we read that "one of his disciples, whom Jesus loved, was reclining at table at Jesus's side" (13:23). Later, the same disciple reappears at the high priest's courtyard after Jesus' arrest (18:15–16), at the scene of the crucifixion (19:35), and at the empty tomb (20:2, 8–9). In these passages this disciple is referred to as "another disciple" (18:15), "he who saw this" (19:35), "the other disciple, the one whom Jesus loved" (20:2), and "the other disciple" (20:8).

The final set of references to the "disciple whom Jesus loved" occur in the accounts of Jesus' third and last resurrection appearance to his disciples (21:7) and Jesus' conversation with the disciple and Peter about their respective future callings (21:20–23). We find the clincher in the penultimate verse of the Gospel: "This is the disciple who is bearing witness about these things, and who has written these things, and we know that his testimony is true" (21:24). Here we are told (in the third-person singular and then first-person plural) that "the disciple whom Jesus loved" and the author of the Gospel, "the disciple who is bearing witness about these things," are one and the same. The Gospel closes with a highly unusual (for a Gospel) first-person reference: "Now there are also many other things that Jesus did. Were every one of them to be written, I *suppose* that the world itself could not contain the books that would be written" (21:25, emphasis added). Upon investigating similar references in ancient literature, I have concluded that this is an epithet of authorial modesty on John's part.[6]

---

6. "I Suppose (*oimai*): The Conclusion of John's Gospel in Its Contemporary Literary and Historical Context," in *The New Testament in Its First Century Setting: Essays on Context and Backgrounds in Honour of B. W. Winter on His 65th Birthday*, ed. P. J. Williams, A. D. Clarke, P. M. Head, and D. Instone-Brewer (Grand Rapids: Eerdmans, 2004), 72–88.

So, the internal evidence from the Gospel itself indicates that it was written by a disciple (1) who was at Jesus' side at the Last Supper (and hence was one of the Twelve); (2) who was at the scene of Jesus' arrest and trial; and (3) who witnessed Jesus' crucifixion and saw Jesus following his resurrection. What an incredible claim the Gospel stakes regarding its author! The seats on either side of Jesus at the Last Supper would have been places of high honor reserved for Jesus' two closest associates—and the author of this Gospel was seated in one of them.

If we were to compare the Gospel of John to a biography of a U.S. president, it wouldn't be something written by a journalist who knows about events in the figure's life only through secondhand accounts or hearsay; it would be written by the president's chief of staff, closest confidant, or another trusted advisor—someone who was by his side at all the major junctures of his presidency.

The "Disciple Whom Jesus Loved" and Peter

There are a few other interesting pieces of information we can gain from the internal evidence. One fascinating datum relates to the numerous passages in John's Gospel where the "disciple whom Jesus loved" appears in close conjunction with Peter.[7] Virtually every time where the "disciple whom Jesus loved" is mentioned in the second half of John's Gospel, Peter is mentioned as well.

- Both are present in the upper room when Peter asks the "disciple whom Jesus loved" to ask about the identity of the betrayer (13:23–24).

- Both are there in the high priest's courtyard; in fact, the "disciple whom Jesus loved" gives Peter access to this courtyard because he is acquainted with the high priest (18:15–16).

---

7. See Kevin Quast, *Peter and the Beloved Disciple: Figures for a Community in Crisis*, LNTS (Sheffield: Sheffield Academic Press, 1989).

- Both visit the empty tomb following Jesus' resurrection; in fact, they run there together. The "disciple whom Jesus loved" (who apparently was the younger of the two) outruns Peter but then respectfully waits for Peter and allows him to peer into the tomb first before he, too, looks inside and sees that the tomb is empty (20:2–9).

- Both are there at the Sea of Galilee, where they see the risen Jesus at the shore. It is only when the "disciple whom Jesus loved" exclaims, "It is the Lord!" that Peter jumps into the lake and swims excitedly toward Jesus (21:7).

- Finally, as mentioned previously, Jesus speaks with Peter and the "disciple whom Jesus loved" at the very end of the Gospel (21:20–23).

Why do we see this consistent parallel characterization of Peter and the "disciple Jesus loved"? And who is the person who best fits this description historically? According to the witness of the other Gospels, the book of Acts, and even Paul's writings, the person who is most closely connected to Peter is the apostle John.

John and Peter, together with John's brother James, make up the inner circle of three who alone witness the raising of Jairus' daughter (Mark 5:37; Luke 8:51), accompany Jesus on the mount of transfiguration (Matt 17:1; Mark 9:2; Luke 9:28), and are taken with him to the garden of Gethsemane (Matt 26:37; Mark 14:33).

In Acts 3, we see Peter and John go to the temple together at the hour of prayer; in Acts 4 both bear witness to the Sanhedrin; and in Acts 8:14–25 they travel together to Samaria to certify the genuineness of Samaritan conversions there. And in Galatians 2:9, Paul calls James (the half-brother of Jesus), Peter (called "Cephas"), and John "pillars" of the church.

So, we see that Peter and John are linked closely in the other Gospels, the book of Acts, and even in Paul's first letter. Therefore, there can be little doubt that in the Fourth Gospel, when Peter is linked consistently with "the disciple whom Jesus loved," that disciple is none other than the apostle John.

Why "Disciple Whom Jesus Loved"?

But why does the apostle John use the unusual phrase "the disciple whom Jesus loved" to identify himself in the Gospel? There are probably multiple reasons. It is likely that he does so to avoid confusion, since there is another person named John featured in this Gospel: John the Baptist. By calling himself simply "the disciple whom Jesus loved," the author reserves the name John for John the Baptist. Thus, when the author first introduces John the Baptist in the Gospel, he simply writes, "There was a man sent from God, whose name was John. He came as a witness, to bear witness about the light ..." (1:6).

We can observe the same phenomenon with regard to another common name, "Mary." Richard Bauckham, who has engaged in an extensive study of personal names in first-century Palestine, conjectures that close to 30 percent of all girls at that time were named either Mary or Salome, with Mary being the most common name.[8] The author of John's Gospel never calls Jesus' mother by the name Mary but instead simply refers to her as "the mother of Jesus" (e.g., 2:1–11). In this way, in John's Gospel, the name Mary is reserved for Mary Magdalene, to whom the author usually refers simply as Mary (e.g., 20:11, 16; cf. 20:18: "Mary Magdalene").

In addition, the phrase "the disciple whom Jesus loved" expresses the important truth that John knew himself to be deeply loved by Jesus. This aligns with his theology and ethic of love, which we can see not only at the footwashing (13:1–20) but also in John's signature verse, John 3:16: "God so loved the world, that he gave his one and only Son, that whoever believes in him should not perish but have

---

8. Richard Bauckham, *Jesus and the Eyewitnesses: The Gospels as Eyewitness Testimony*, 2nd ed. (Grand Rapids: Eerdmans, 2017), 39–92, drawing on Tal Ilan, *Lexicon of Jewish Names in Late Antiquity: Part I: Palestine 330 BCE–200 CE*, Texts and Studies in Ancient Judaism 91 (Tübingen: Mohr-Siebeck, 2002).

eternal life." The most important truth John believed was that he was an undeserving recipient of Jesus' redeeming love.[9]

NOBODY BETTER

If you were looking for someone to write the fourth, final Gospel to be included in the New Testament, you couldn't have found anyone better than the apostle John. In fact, despite his characteristic authorial modesty, which is on display both in the humble title "the disciple whom Jesus loved" and in the concluding phrase "I suppose" in the last verse of the Gospel, this is exactly the claim John himself stakes in the Gospel.

Let's look at a startling verbal similarity that makes an astonishing assertion regarding John's closeness to Jesus. Structurally, John's Gospel neatly and symmetrically breaks down into two roughly equal halves, often called "The Book of Signs" (John 1–12) and "The Book of Glory" or "The Book of Exaltation" (John 13–20); these two halves are framed by a prologue (1:1–18) and an epilogue (John 21). In his prologue, John says regarding Jesus, "No one has ever seen God; the only God, *who is at the Father's side* [Grk. *eis ton kolpon*], he has made him known" (1:18, emphasis added). In John 13, which kicks off the second half of the Gospel, the stage is set for the Last Supper: Jesus washes the disciples' feet and then reclines at supper with his closest followers. John tells us that "one of his disciples, whom Jesus loved, was reclining at table *at Jesus' side*" (13:23, emphasis added). The Greek expression translated "at Jesus' side," *en tō kolpō*, is an almost exact verbal parallel to the description of Jesus being "at the Father's side" in the prologue (1:18). Coincidence? Hardly. Especially since at the end of the Gospel, John writes, "Peter turned and saw the disciple whom Jesus loved following them, the one who also had leaned back against [his chest; Grk. *epi to stēthos*]

9. See "The Johannine Love Ethic," in Andreas J. Köstenberger, *A Theology of John's Gospel and Letters: The Word, the Christ, the Son of God*, BTNT (Grand Rapids: Zondervan, 2009), ch. 13.

during the supper and had said, 'Lord, who is it that is going to betray you?' " (21:20).

John is thus deliberately casting the "disciple whom Jesus loved"—himself—in a position parallel to none other than Jesus. Specifically, he is implying that the way in which *Jesus* was closely and intimately related to God the *Father* resembles the way in which he, *John*, was closely and intimately related to *Jesus*. This closeness to God the Father, in turn, put Jesus in an ideal position to explain God and to give a full account of him, just as John's proximity to Jesus put him in an ideal position to explain Jesus and to give a full account of him. That's an astonishing claim!

Add to this the fact that, as we saw in the previous chapter, John is regularly featured alongside the apostle Peter in the second half of the Gospel. The Synoptic Gospels present Peter as the preeminent spokesman of the Twelve and the one to whom Jesus gave the keys to the kingdom of heaven. In John's Gospel, however, John shows his own preeminence when it comes to his spiritual insight and closeness to Jesus.

At the Last Supper, Peter asks the "disciple whom Jesus loved" (who is at Jesus' side) to ask Jesus about the identity of the betrayer (13:23–24). Later, it is again Peter who asks "the other disciple" to help him gain access to the high priest's courtyard, and that disciple is able to do so because he was known to the high priest's family (18:15–16).[10] Then, on resurrection day, when Peter and the "disciple whom Jesus loved" run to the empty tomb, John outruns Peter (though he respectfully waits for him and lets him peer into the tomb

---

10. The scholar Michael Bird's protestations notwithstanding—"If you are about to adjudicate a case against a possible enemy of the state, you don't let in your fishmonger!"—the apostle John was not your ordinary fishmonger! Contra Michael F. Bird, "Authorship of the Fourth Gospel Revisited," *Patheos*, March 2, 2020, https://www.patheos.com/blogs/euangelion/2020/03/authorship-of-the-fourth-gospel-revisited, referring to a recent discussion of the authorship of John's Gospel. For his part, Bird, along with his co-author N. T. Wright, concludes, "the 'John' behind the gospel … was probably John the elder, a Judean disciple of Jesus, not one of the Twelve." See N. T. Wright and Michael F. Bird, *The New Testament in Its World: An Introduction to the History, Literature, and Theology of the First Christians* (Grand Rapids: Zondervan, 2019), esp. 648–52.

first; 20:8–9). In John 21, it is the "disciple whom Jesus loved" who first recognizes the risen Jesus, at which Peter jumps into the lake to swim toward Jesus (20:7). The parallel characterization of Peter and John comes to a climax in the final scene of the Gospel where Jesus recommissions Peter three times after Peter had denied him three times. Subsequently, when Jesus tells Peter that he will die a martyr's death, Peter asks Jesus, "But what about John?" In response, Jesus tells Peter, in so many words, to mind his own business.[11]

In each of the five scenes in which John and Peter are featured together, it is John who possesses unique spiritual insight or access to Jesus and becomes the gateway through which others can gain such insight and access. This reinforces the parallelism between the evangelist's characterization of Jesus in relation to the Father on the one hand and of John in relation to Jesus on the other. The bottom line is this: no one was closer to Jesus during his earthly ministry than John. For this reason, no Gospel presents Jesus' person and work in a more perceptive and spiritually penetrating manner than does the Fourth Gospel. I believe this is what Clement of Alexandria meant when he wrote that "John, last of all, composed a spiritual Gospel."

It does indeed matter who wrote John's Gospel. John had known Jesus like no other; he loved Jesus more than anything; and he wanted to share that love and spiritual insight with others who had not had the privilege of knowing Jesus personally during his earthly ministry. When he wrote the Gospel, John was in his eighties and had seen many of his fellow apostles and other Christians die a martyr's death in witnessing to their Christian faith. He had seen the Roman Empire persecute Christians, herd them into the Coliseum, and feed them to the lions as in a circus. But he had also seen the success of the early Christian mission; Christianity—belief in Jesus as Messiah—had spread from Jerusalem and Judea to Samaria and the ends of the earth.

---

11. Though note that, similar to the parallel characterization of John in relation to Jesus, the author also features Peter in terms parallel to Jesus: just like Jesus, Peter would die a martyr's death and glorify God by giving his life for his faith (21:19; cf. 12:33).

He may even have seen incipient forms of the heresy of Gnosticism, which diminished Jesus' humanity or deity or both. Perhaps this is why he insisted so adamantly that Jesus was the eternal, pre-existent Word become flesh.

EXTERNAL EVIDENCE

I could list additional internal evidence, but hopefully what I've presented thus far has convinced you that the internal evidence points unequivocally to the apostle John as the author of the Gospel. Let's now turn to the external evidence.

I started with the internal evidence and have surveyed it at some length because I believe the internal evidence is in some ways more important and decisive than the external evidence in that it is embedded in the canonical, inspired, and inerrant text of the Gospel itself. Nevertheless, the external evidence carries some weight as well, and, in this case, the internal and external evidence converge.

Perhaps the first piece of external evidence I should mention is the title "The Gospel according to John." While this could refer to a John other than the apostle, this is highly unlikely, since no other John mentioned in any of the Gospels had anywhere near the stature of the apostle John, the son of Zebedee, who was one of the Twelve.

The second piece of external evidence is that virtually all the earliest church fathers refer to the apostle John as the author of the Gospel. For example, Irenaeus of Lyons (AD 130–200) wrote, "John the disciple of the Lord, who leaned back on his breast, published the Gospel while he was a resident at Ephesus in Asia" (*Heresies* 3.1.2). Irenaeus thus linked the authorship of John's Gospel directly to "the disciple whom Jesus loved" who is mentioned in John 13:23 as being present at the Lord's Supper. Similarly, Clement of Alexandria (AD 150–215) wrote, "Last of all, John ... composed a spiritual Gospel" (quoted by Eusebius, *Ecclesiastical History* 6.14.7). So, we see that the earliest church fathers, who in some cases had a direct connection with the apostle John (e.g., Irenaeus was a student of Polycarp, who was a student of John), attributed authorship of the Gospel to him.[12] It wasn't until the late eighteenth century that a small group of scholars began to question the apostolic authorship of John's Gospel. However, many of their doubts, expressed in works written between 1790 and 1810, were not well supported by the historical evidence. Often, they were based on tenuous philosophical, theological, or ideological presuppositions.[13]

Defenders of apostolic authorship ably refuted all the arguments advanced against apostolic authorship. Nevertheless, today, scholars who believe that the apostle John wrote the Gospel are in the minority—not because the historical evidence is lacking, but because critical scholarship has been increasingly biased against traditional authorship of the Gospels and the New Testament letters as part of a reaction against the established church and an antipathy toward taking Scripture at face value.[14]

RECENT SCHOLARSHIP

I have interacted extensively with recent scholars who dispute the apostolic authorship of John's Gospel such as Martin Hengel, Richard Bauckham, Ben Witherington, Robert Kysar, and many others. Martin Hengel, a leading German New Testament scholar and historian, speaks of a Johannine *Doppelantlitz*, that is, a "dual face." By this, he acknowledges that the internal evidence points toward apostolic authorship but argues that, while the author wants his readers to believe the apostle John wrote the Gospel, he didn't in fact write it. Rather, Hengel argues that the actual author of the Gospel was John

---

12. Cf. Irenaeus, *Against Heresies* 3.3.

13. See my article "Frühe Zweifel an der johanneischen Verfasserschaft des vierten Evangeliums in der modernen Interpretationsgeschichte," *European Journal of Theology* 5 (1996): 37–46; "Early Doubts of the Apostolic Authorship of the Fourth Gospel in the History of Modern Biblical Criticism," in *Studies in John and Gender: A Decade of Scholarship*, Studies in Biblical Literature (New York: Peter Lang, 2001).

14. You can read more about this in chap. 1 in *The Cradle, the Cross, and the Crown* as well as in the introduction to *A Theology of John's Gospel and Letters*.

the elder, a figure of whom virtually nothing is known other than a passing reference in one of the church father Papias' writings, which is now lost but has come down to us in the writings of the church historian Eusebius.[15]

Similarly, in his important book *Jesus and the Eyewitnesses*, Richard Bauckham defends the eyewitness nature of the biblical Gospels in general but at the same time inexplicably denies both Matthean and Johannine authorship. Similar to Hengel, Bauckham believes a member of the Jerusalem aristocracy, perhaps the host of the Last Supper, a man by the name of John (John the elder?), wrote the Gospel.[16] Ben Witherington, a prolific Wesleyan scholar who teaches at Asbury Seminary, believes Lazarus wrote the Gospel,[17] while others, as mentioned, posit an anonymous Johannine community. Interestingly, though, some adherents of the Johannine community hypothesis, such as Robert Kysar, have changed their minds and now advocate a postmodern reading of the Gospel.

Why do we find this almost inexplicable aversion to apostolic authorship, even by otherwise competent historians such as Hengel or Bauckham? It seems that some underlying presuppositions are at work that preclude apostolic authorship at the very outset, without giving adequate consideration to the actual historical evidence for apostolic authorship, both internal and external. Apostolic authorship is typically ruled out *a priori* as a possible option. No wonder critical scholars conclude that someone other than the apostle John wrote the Gospel!

---

15. See my review of Martin Hengel, *Die johanneische Frage*, *JETS* 39 (1996): 154–55.

16. Bauckham believes the apostle John, if he had been the author, would not obliquely refer to the "sons of Zebedee," as he does in 21:2. However, I don't think this is as insurmountable an objection as Bauckham makes it out to be, as ancient authors frequently referred to themselves in the third person. Note, for example, that Jesus refers to himself in the third person as "Jesus Christ whom you have sent" in his final prayer (17:3). See Bauckham, *Jesus and the Eyewitnesses*, 412–71.

17. Ben Witherington, "Was Lazarus the Beloved Disciple?" *Ben Witherington* (blog), January 9, 2007, http://benwitherington. blogspot.com/2007/01/was-lazarus-beloved-disciple.html.

Sadly, it is virtually impossible in today's intellectual climate to hold to apostolic Johannine authorship and to be respected and accepted by mainstream academic scholarship.[18] But then, to paraphrase the apostle Paul, it is a small thing to be rejected by mainstream academia; the only thing that matters in the end is that we are approved by God as those who accurately handle his word of truth (1 Cor 4:3–4; 2 Tim 2:15).

CONCLUSION ON AUTHORSHIP

Hopefully, I have proven sufficiently and beyond reasonable doubt for our purposes that the apostle John wrote the Gospel that bears his name. This will be an important foundation for the remainder of this volume for the following reasons.

1. It will clarify what we are talking about when we speak of "John's theology." We are talking about the theology of the apostle John, who was the closest eyewitness to Jesus during his earthly ministry.

2. A firm belief in apostolic Johannine authorship will provide us with a strong positive conviction as to the authority, accuracy, and reliability of John's witness, especially in a Gospel that highly prizes eyewitness testimony.

3. We have a solid basis for affirming that the theology conveyed in John's Gospel is coherent and flows out of intimate personal acquaintance with its main subject, the Lord Jesus Christ, and the experience of following him closely in discipleship.

---

18. Incidentally, there are a few fascinating paragraphs on this in Leon Morris's excellent volume *Studies in the Fourth Gospel* (Grand Rapids: Eerdmans, 1969), where he voices similar concerns. You can read up on this in my essay, "Leon Morris's Scholarship on John's Gospel: An Assessment and Critical Reflection on His Scholarship," in *The Gospel of John in Modern Interpretation*, Milestones in New Testament Scholarship, ed. Stanley E. Porter and Ron C. Fay (Grand Rapids: Kregel, 2018), 197–209.

While some would consider this a liability and allege that any personal commitment to the subject of one's work automatically results in bias and inaccuracy, I would disagree. It is possible to be strongly invested in a subject and to be passionate about it and yet, precisely because one is passionate about a subject, to be committed to accurate reporting. If anyone is detached and dispassionate in their writing and thinking about a person like Jesus who staked such astonishing claims regarding himself, it makes me wonder if they really understand who he claimed to be and how earth-shattering the significance of his coming is.

JOHN'S PROLOGUE

In the following two chapters, I'll walk us through the Cana Cycle in John's Gospel, which comprises John 2–4. But for the remainder of this chapter, I would like us to take a brief look at the prologue to John's Gospel, which is of supreme importance in understanding where John is going in his Gospel and how John's Gospel is distinctive and unique.[19]

John's prologue is vital for understanding his Gospel as a whole. The prologue gives us the lens through which to view John's entire presentation of Jesus in the remainder of the Gospel. To provide a framework for our study of John's prologue, here is a possible outline that shows that John most likely structured the prologue using a chiastic construction, ABCB'A':[20]

---

19. P. J. Williams, "Not the Prologue of John," *JSNT* 33 (2011): 375–86, helpfully points out that the earliest manuscripts of John's Gospel treat John 1:1–5, not John 1:1–18, as the introduction to John's Gospel. As a result, he eschews calling John 1:1–18 "John's prologue." But such scholarly squabbles need not detain us here.

20. I am indebted here to the work of the very astute Johannine literary scholar R. Alan Culpepper and his article, "The Pivot of John's Prologue," *NTS* 27 (1980): 1–31.

FIG. 1: CHIASTIC STRUCTURE OF JOHN'S PROLOGUE
(JOHN 1:1–18)

A: The Word's Activity in Creation (1:1–5)

    B: John's Witness Concerning the Light (1:6–8)

        C: The Incarnation of the Word & the
        Privilege of Becoming God's Children (1:9–14)

    B': John's Witness Concerning the Word's
    Preeminence (1:15)

A': The Final Revelation Brought by Jesus Christ (1:16–18)

This could be a helpful outline as you teach or preach through the prologue. You could go through it in linear fashion, verse by verse, or you could start with verses 1–5, then go to the corresponding bookend, verses 16–18; after this, cover verses 6–8 and 15 about John the Baptist; and conclude with the center of the prologue, verses 9–14, which deal with the incarnation of the Word and the privilege of becoming God's children by faith in Christ.

THE INCARNATE WORD

John opens his Gospel with the well-known words, "In the beginning was the Word, and the Word was with God, and the Word was God. He was in the beginning with God" (1:1–2). This is an incredibly momentous declaration, with its opening allusion to the first verse in the book of Genesis. You can see right out of the gate why many believe that John has an exceedingly high Christology. Here John is saying that before Jesus was born and placed in a manger in Bethlehem, he preexisted eternally with God the Father. In fact, it was through Jesus—the preincarnate Word—that God spoke the created universe into being (1:3–4).

What is more, not only does John call the preincarnate Jesus "the Word" and identify him as the agent of creation, but he also identifies Jesus as "God" (Grk. *theos*) on par with God the Father, the

Creator and Yahweh, God of Israel. The opening words of John's prologue heavily influenced the church's doctrinal formulation of the Trinity, the deity of Christ, and Christology in the early centuries of the Christian era. In many ways, we owe to John an immeasurable theological and Christological debt as he considerably deepened the presentation of Jesus as virgin-born, preexistent, and divine in the other (Synoptic) Gospels.

This same preexistent Word through whom God spoke creation into being, John argues, subsequently became flesh in Jesus, who "pitched his tent" among his people (Grk. *skenoō*, 1:14; our word "skin" derives from this word). John and his fellow apostles perceived his glory (Grk. *theaomai*, a more specific word than the Greek word for simply seeing; it is a precursor of our word "theater").

The glory the apostles perceived in Jesus, John continues, is that of the one and only Son—the unique, one-of-a-kind Son—of the Father, full of grace and truth (1:14). Here we see a reference to Jesus as the eschatological (end-time) manifestation of God's presence in the midst of his people. This is in continuity with previous divine manifestations in the tabernacle and later the temple, which, Scripture tells us, was filled with God's glory in Solomon's time:

> As soon as Solomon finished his prayer, fire came down from heaven and consumed the burnt offering and the sacrifices, and the glory of the LORD filled the temple. And the priests could not enter the house of the LORD, because the glory of the LORD filled the LORD's house. When all the people of Israel saw the fire come down and the glory of the LORD on the temple, they bowed down with their faces to the ground on the pavement and worshiped and gave thanks to the LORD, saying, "For he is good, for his steadfast love endures forever." (1 Chr 7:1–3; see also 1 Kgs 8:11; 2 Chr 5:14)

John tells us that in Jesus, God's glory had come to earth in all its fullness, and from this fullness, God's people had all received "grace instead of grace" (John 1:16; translations like ESV render this phrase "grace upon grace," but I prefer the translation "grace instead of grace" because the preposition is *anti*, "instead of," not *epi*, "upon").

John continues, "For the law was given through Moses, grace and truth came through Jesus Christ" (1:17). In other words, the law was good, but Jesus is better—so much better! Moses asked to see God's glory, but God told him he would not be able to see him and live (Exod 33:18–23). By contrast, John tells us in the last verse of the prologue that while "no one has ever seen God; the only God, who is at the Father's side, he has made him known" (1:18).

JOHN'S SENDING CHRISTOLOGY

Jesus, who eternally preexisted with God the Father, "has made him known"; he came to give a "full account" of God the Father (Grk. *exēgeomai*; a loose paraphrase might be that Jesus has "exegeted" the Father). In this way, John tells us that we should read the rest of the Gospel as Jesus giving a full account of what God is like and to see both Jesus' works (especially his signs) and his words (his discourses) as a manifestation of God's glory.

As we'll see in the next chapter, John concludes his account of Jesus performing his first sign at the wedding at Cana by saying that when Jesus revealed his glory, "his disciples believed in him" (2:11). Later, in the upper room, Jesus' follower Philip asks Jesus to show him the Father; Jesus responds almost as if Philip hurt his feelings by even asking the question:

> Have I been with you so long, and you still do not know me, Philip? Whoever has seen me has seen the Father. How can you say, "Show us the Father"? Do you not believe that I am in the Father and the Father is in me? The words that I say to you I do not speak on my own authority, but the Father who dwells in me does his works. Believe me that I am in the Father and the Father is in me, or else believe on account of the works themselves. (14:9–11)

John's entire sending Christology is encapsulated in the unity between Jesus the Word and God the Father. This is most likely due to Isaiah's influence, particularly his depiction of God's word in Isaiah 55:10–11:

> For as the rain and the snow come down from heaven
>   and do not return there but water the earth,
> making it bring forth and sprout,
>   giving seed to the sower and bread to the eater,
> so shall my word be that goes out from my mouth;
>   it shall not return to me empty,
> but it shall accomplish that which I purpose,
>   and shall succeed in the thing for which I sent it.

CHILDREN OF GOD

I've saved the best for last. If John's prologue is constructed in the form of a chiasm, at the very center of the chiasm is not the incarnation, the Word-become-flesh in Jesus, as important as this affirmation is both theologically and Christologically. Rather, the central affirmation in John's prologue is found in verse 12, where John writes, "He came to his own, and his own people did not receive him. But to all who did receive him, who believed in his name, he gave the right to become children of God, who were born, not of blood nor of the will of the flesh nor of the will of man, but of God" (1:11–13).

Therefore, the central affirmation, which has supreme relevance for all of humanity, is that "to all who did receive Jesus, who believed in his name, he gave the right to become children of God"—to be reborn spiritually by God. As we'll see, Jesus develops this truth further in his conversation with Nicodemus, the teacher of Israel, in John 3. But John states this vital spiritual truth at the very outset of his Gospel. If we believe in Jesus' name, we are given the right to become God's children! In Old Testament times, God's chosen people were the people of Israel, but now this privilege has been extended to anyone who believes in Jesus (3:16). Can anything be more important?

Later in John's Gospel, when people ask Jesus, "What must we do, to be doing the works of God?" Jesus answers, "This is the work of God, that you believe in him whom he has sent" (6:28–29). As always, Jesus' answer is simple yet incredibly profound. People were looking for works they could accomplish for God. But Jesus said that the only "work of God"—the only work God requires of any of us—is to believe in the one whom he has sent, the Lord Jesus Christ. To believe, or not to believe, that is the question. It is so simple yet so profound.

That's one of the many things I love about John's Gospel. He reduces everything to the central question with which each one of us is confronted. It's as if John wrote his entire Gospel as an answer to the question Jesus asked his disciples in the other three Gospels: "Who do you say that I am?" (Matt 10:15; Mark 8:29; Luke 9:20). John gives his answer in his purpose statement at the end of his Gospel: "Now Jesus did many other signs in the presence of the disciples, which are not written in this book; but these are written so that you may believe that Jesus is the Christ, the Son of God, and that by believing you may have life in his name" (John 20:30–31). How does John make his case? To repurpose Jesus' words to his first followers, "Come and see" (1:39 NRSV).

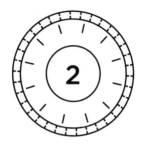

THE CANA CYCLE

PART 1

*The Cana Wedding and
the Temple Clearing
(John 2)*

—

I n the first chapter, I made a case for the apostolic authorship of John's Gospel—that is, I proposed that the author of the Fourth Gospel was none other than the apostle John. I argued that both internal evidence in the Gospel itself and external evidence supports this notion. If I and almost 1,800 years of church history, not to mention the claims embedded in the Gospel itself, am correct, the author was a man who knew Jesus extremely well, probably better than anyone else ever knew him. That's incredible. We shouldn't lose sight of that in the hubbub of the scholarly squabble about Johannine authorship.

During Jesus' earthly ministry, John would have been about thirty years old; tradition has it that he was the youngest disciple. Artists often depicted John with effeminate features, as artists in certain artistic periods commonly did when portraying youths. Dan Brown, the author of the *Da Vinci Code*, cleverly suggested that the individual at Jesus' side with effeminate features in Leonardo da Vinci's *The Last Supper* was not the apostle John but a woman, Mary Magdalene, who allegedly was Jesus' wife.[1] Later, Karen King of Harvard University claimed to have identified what she called "The Gospel of Jesus's Wife." However, she later admitted that this document was forged and inauthentic.[2]

In any case, John was quite young during Jesus' earthly ministry, and he was apparently rather zealous. In an episode recorded

---

1. Dan Brown, *The Da Vinci Code* (New York: Doubleday, 2003). For an assessment, see Andreas J. Köstenberger, *The Da Vinci Code: Is Christianity True?* (Wake Forest, NC: Southeastern Baptist Theological Seminary, 2006), https://s3.amazonaws.com/5mt.bf.org/2017/10/1-Da-Vinci-Booklet.pdf.

2. Ariel Sabar, "Karen King Responds to 'Unbelievable Tale of Jesus's Wife,'" *The Atlantic*, June 16, 2016, https://www.theatlantic.com/politics/archive/2016/06/karen-king-responds-to-the-unbelievable-tale-of-jesus-wife/487484.

in Luke, John and his (likely older) brother James asked Jesus if he wanted them to call down fire from heaven when some Samaritans didn't allow them passage through their territory (Luke 9:54). This earned the sons of Zebedee the playful nickname *Boanerges*, which means "sons of thunder" (Mark 3:17).

When he was writing his Gospel, John was half a century older and no doubt a lot wiser than he was in the Gospel account; he was probably in his eighties. He had half a century to reflect on his experience of following the earthly Jesus and to ponder the significance of what had happened. He also had the benefit of several other Gospels being published, which presented in more pedestrian fashion—though still with great theological acuity—the string of events that took place during Jesus' earthly ministry, as well as much of his teaching.

In this and the next chapter, we'll study the Cana Cycle, which spans John 2–4. The designation Cana Cycle derives from the fact that this literary unit of John's Gospel starts and ends with signs Jesus performed in the small village of Cana in the Galilean north. In this chapter, we'll look at the first two units, in which Jesus turns water into wine and clears the temple. In the next chapter, we'll look at Jesus' conversations with Nicodemus and the Samaritan woman as well as his healing of the gentile centurion's son, which completes the Cana Cycle. If you're teaching or preaching through John's Gospel, consider using the following outline:

FIG. 2: STRUCTURE OF CANA CYCLE (JOHN 2–4)

1. Turning Water into Wine: Jesus' First Cana Sign (2:1–12)
2. Clearing the Temple: A Jerusalem Sign (2:13–22)
3. Jesus' Conversation with Nicodemus (2:23–3:21)[3]
4. Jesus' Conversation with the Samaritan Woman (4:1–45)
5. Healing the Centurion's Son: Second Sign in Cana (4:46–54)

RELATIONSHIP TO THE
OTHER GOSPELS

Before we delve into John 2, let's take a moment to situate John's Gospel in relation to the other Gospels. As you look at the five passages listed above, you'll begin to realize just how unique John's Gospel really is. Matthew and Luke include accounts of the virgin birth of Jesus; the Sermon on the Mount (or Plain), including the Lord's Prayer; Jesus' teaching on the kingdom of God, especially numerous kingdom parables; and Jesus' Olivet Discourse on the end times. Matthew and Luke also include a final commissioning of disciples: Matthew ends with the Great Commission, while Luke records the commissioning and then goes on to write a whole additional volume, the book of Acts.

John doesn't include any of these things: no virgin birth, no Sermon on the Mount, no Lord's Prayer, no teaching on God's kingdom, no parables, no demon exorcisms, and no end-time discourse. Instead, he features seven signs that Jesus performed, as well as seven witnesses to Jesus and seven "I am" sayings. Do you get the idea that he likes the number seven? He also features Jesus as the preexistent Word become flesh. In addition, he features the Farewell Discourse, which is utterly unique and includes Jesus' final prayer (sometimes called the high priestly prayer).

---

3. The material in 3:22–36 covers Jesus' movement from Jerusalem to the Judean country-side and John the Baptist's witness to Jesus. This could be covered either in a separate message or be briefly addressed at the end of a message or lesson about Jesus' conversation with Nicodemus in 2:23–3:21.

Along the way, John helps his readers discover many ironies and misunderstandings during the course of Jesus' ministry. He presents the entire story of Jesus as a grand cosmic battle against the powers of darkness, in particular Satan, the "ruler of this world" (12:31). He is insistent that Jesus' glory is evident not only at the transfiguration but *throughout* his ministry and states that those who believe in him have *already* passed from death to life (scholars call this John's "realized eschatology"). So, while John omits an awful lot that the Synoptics cover, he also adds a great deal of new material, not to mention beloved characters (some of whom we'll be talking about in the next chapter) such as Nicodemus, the Samaritan woman, the man born blind, and Lazarus.

Because John's Gospel shows so little overlap with the three earlier New Testament Gospels, scholars debate whether John knew about them and, if so, whether he had read them. The critical scholarly consensus today is that John wrote independently of the other Gospels (a radical independence view), which is a reaction against the traditional understanding that John did know the Synoptic accounts but chose to write his own Gospel.[4]

However, a radical independence view is highly implausible.[5] As we can see from Acts and the New Testament epistles, the early Christian movement was a close-knit network, a "holy internet," as one writer has called it.[6] I find it almost unimaginable that someone of the apostle John's stature—or anyone interested in the Christian movement, for that matter—would have been unaware of the existence of several earlier Gospels. I find it even less plausible that, if he knew of their existence, John would not have wanted to read them before writing his own Gospel.

---

4. The emergence of the radical independence view can be traced back to a short book by Percival Gardner-Smith, *Saint John and the Synoptic Gospels* (Cambridge: Cambridge University Press, 1938).

5. See my article...

6. Michael B. Thompson, "The Holy Internet: Communication Between Churches in the First Christian Generation," in *The Gospels for All Christians*, ed. Richard J. Bauckham (Grand Rapids: Eerdmans, 1998), 49–70.

You may be asking: If John knew the other Gospels, why did he make so little use of them? That's a fair question. My answer is this: theological transposition. John was not content merely to restate what the earlier Gospels had already competently and accurately set forth. Rather, he assumed much of the content of the earlier Gospels and theologically transposed various motifs to bring out the underlying significance of particular aspects of Jesus' person or work, just like in music you may transpose a tune into a different key.

Take Jesus' miracles, for example.[7] The word used for "miracle" in Matthew, Mark, and Luke is *dynamis*, meaning "powerful work." The focus in those Gospels is on Jesus' authority over the natural and supernatural world, including sickness, the natural realm, and the demonic. The only "sign" of his authority Jesus gives to those who oppose him is the "sign of Jonah"—being in the belly of the big fish for three days and three nights, which, Jesus implies, foreshadows his own crucifixion and resurrection after three days.

But John never uses the word *dynamis*, "powerful work." Instead he selects seven messianic signs of Jesus:

FIG. 3: THE SEVEN SIGNS OF JESUS IN JOHN'S GOSPEL
(JOHN 2–12)

1. turning water into wine at the Cana wedding (2:1–12)
2. clearing the temple in Jerusalem (2:13–22)
3. healing the gentile centurion's son (4:46–54; three signs in Cana Cycle)
4. healing the lame man in Jerusalem (5:1–15)
5. feeding the five thousand in Galilee (6:1–15)
6. healing the man born blind (John 9; three signs in Festival Cycle)
7. raising of Lazarus, foreshadowing Jesus' resurrection (John 11)

---

7. If you want more, see the following article where I list as many as twenty Johannine transpositions: "John's Transposition Theology: Retelling the Story of Jesus in a Different Key," in *Earliest Christian History: History, Literature, and Theology; Essays from the Tyndale Fellowship in Honor of Martin Hengel*, ed. Michael F. Bird and Jason Maston; WUNT 2/320 (Tübingen: Mohr-Siebeck, 2012), 191–226.

This theological and terminological recasting, I believe, is anything but coincidental; in all probability, it is deliberate and gives us a fascinating glimpse into John's thought. John's seminal insight is that Jesus' miracles are not primarily a display of his power but a demonstration of his messianic identity. In other words, people may have marveled at Jesus' dazzling ability to transform water into wine or to raise a man who had been in the tomb for four days and was already exuding a strong odor from death, but they may still have missed the ultimate purpose of that particular feat—namely, to lead them to believe that the Messiah, the Son of God, had come in Jesus.

Remember John's purpose statement? "Now Jesus did many other signs in the presence of the disciples, which are not written in this book [in other words, John was highly selective; compare the other Gospels]; but these are written so that you may believe that Jesus is the Christ, the Son of God, and that by believing you may have life in his name" (20:30–31). The miracles are messianic signs! To miss their significance—the way they point to Jesus' true identity as the God-sent Messiah and Son of God—is to miss the very purpose for which they were intended.

So what the Synoptic Gospels present as evidence for Jesus' comprehensive authority as the messenger of God's kingdom—as Jesus says in Matthew 28:18, "All authority in heaven and on earth has been given to me"—John presents as signs, acts pointing beyond themselves to who Jesus is.

That's what brilliant theologians do: help us see the significance of certain vital events in deeper ways. Now don't get me wrong, I believe all four Gospels were written by men who were historically, literarily, and theologically competent and highly astute. But I believe John's Gospel comes at the apex, at the very peak of revealing the purpose of Jesus' coming and redemptive work, as John could build on the material presented in the earlier Gospels, wrote a generation after them, and was the disciple who had been the closest to Jesus during his earthly ministry.

THE CANA CYCLE (PART 1)

Let's now turn to the Cana Cycle, which covers John 2–4. This is a good example of John's tendency to break new ground rather than merely repeating information found in the other Gospels. Those earlier Gospels do not even mention Cana or Jesus' turning of water into wine. Neither do they mention Jesus' conversations with Nicodemus, the teacher of Israel, and the Samaritan woman, which are at the heart of the Cana Cycle. So, we have in John 2–4 rather unique material.

There is some overlap, such as the clearing of the temple—though even this is debated. The earlier three Gospels show Jesus cleansing the temple during his final week of ministry just prior to his crucifixion.[8] John's Gospel, however, shows Jesus doing so at the very *beginning* of his ministry, the first time he travels to Jerusalem for the annual Passover. Is this another example of theological transposition?

Some, such as Craig Keener, who wrote a two-volume commentary on John's Gospel, say John here engages in historical and literary transposition—that is, he transferred an event that historically happened at the *end* of Jesus' ministry to the *beginning* for theological reasons.[9] Personally, I doubt this is the case. When you look at the way John tells the story, the time markers are very tight. In John 2:12 he says, "After this he [Jesus] went down to Capernaum, with his mother and his brothers and his disciples, and they stayed there for a few days." And then, in John 2:13, he says, "The Passover of the Jews was at hand, and Jesus went up to Jerusalem." John gives every indication that he tells the story chronologically. I believe history and theology go together. You can't easily elevate theology and sacrifice history in order to do so. Good theology respects history rather than changing or overriding it.

For this and other reasons, I believe it is more likely that John knew of an earlier time in which Jesus cleansed the temple—a temple cleansing in addition to the one recorded in the earlier Gospels—and

---

8. Matthew 21:12–17 // Mark 11:15–19 // Luke 19:45–48.

9. Craig S. Keener, *John*, 2 vols. (Peabody, MA: Hendrickson, 2003), 1:518.

chose to include the former rather than the latter. Why would he do that? He likely wanted to make room for the raising of Lazarus, the seventh sign of Jesus, at the climax of his narrative. In the earlier Gospels, the temple cleansing is that climax—the final straw that broke the camel's back. Jesus frontally challenged the authority of the Jewish leaders who were in charge of temple worship and the sacrificial system, and it became clear that there was going to be a head-on collision between their conflicting interests and claims. I believe that John—supplementing rather than contradicting the earlier Gospels—makes clear that Jesus challenged the temple establishment not just at the very end of his ministry but from the very beginning.

THE WEDDING AT CANA:
JESUS' FIRST MESSIANIC SIGN (2:1–12)

Let us now look at the beginning of the Cana Cycle, the wedding at Cana. This is Jesus' first of seven signs in the first half of his Gospel, the Book of Signs (John 1–12). In John 1, following the prologue, John essentially begins to narrate Jesus' first week of ministry. The narrative breaks down neatly into several days, each of which is introduced by the phrase "the next day" (1:29, 35, 43). The wedding at Cana is introduced by the phrase "On the third day" (2:1). On one level, this completes the first week of Jesus' ministry. On another level, John may see here a parallel with creation week as part of the "new creation" motif in John's Gospel.[10] Also, John may be hinting at Jesus' resurrection, which also happened "on the third day" (cf. 2:19, 20; though 20:1 refers to it as taking place on "the first day of the week").

John then mentions a wedding that took place at Cana in Galilee. The corresponding bookend to this is 4:46, which says, "So he came

---

10. For further details, see my *Theology of John's Gospel*, 336–54. Note that, most likely, the wedding is here (implicitly) narrated as taking place on the Sabbath, the seventh day of the week (and the third day after the previous event narrated in John's Gospel took place). This, however, is set in the context of a Jewish wedding feast, which normally lasted for several days or even an entire week. See my contribution on John's Gospel in J. Scott Duvall and J. Daniel Hays, *Baker Illustrated Bible Background Commentary* (Grand Rapids: Baker, 2020).

again to Cana in Galilee, where he had made the water wine" (one of
John's many helpful back references; cf. 7:50; 18:14; 19:39; 21:20). John
himself draws the reader's attention to the fact that Jesus has come
full circle, as it were, and that he has returned to where he started his
ministry, the little Galilean village of Cana.[11]

Notice that, in the account of the Cana wedding in John 2, the only
named character is Jesus. Jesus' mother, his disciples, the groom and
bride, the master of the banquet, and the servants all remain unnamed.
In naming Jesus alone, John identifies him as the main character. The
scene becomes the occasion at which a facet of Jesus' messianic mission is revealed—namely, that he is the bringer of great eschatological joy, which is symbolized by the abundance of wine; and yet, his
time has not yet come. This Jesus' mother fails to understand, which
is why Jesus' reply to her request is rather firm: "Woman, what does
this have to do with me? My hour has not yet come" (2:4). As far as I
know, this is the only ancient literary evidence we have where a man
calls his mother "woman."

Interestingly, Jesus' mother is undaunted—a tribute to her strong
faith in Jesus—and simply tells the servants, "Do whatever he tells
you" (2:5). This echoes Pharaoh's words to the Egyptians in Genesis
41:55 regarding Joseph during a severe famine. Through this parallel, John wants us to draw a salvation-historical connection between
Joseph's help in times of famine and Jesus' help in times of spiritual
famine in Israel. Running out of wine serves as a sort of parable for

---

11. In 4:54, the Cana Cycle helpfully closes with the note, "This was now the second
sign that Jesus did when he had come from Judea into Galilee." Many, incidentally, take this
to mean that there are no intervening signs between the turning of water into wine in John 2
and the healing of the centurion's son in John 4, but I believe that 4:54 refers only to signs in
Cana. In 2:23 and 3:2, however, you'll find two additional references to Jesus' signs performed
in Jerusalem, and I believe that the clearing of the temple is in fact such a messianic sign. If
so, there are actually three signs narrated in the Cana Cycle, the two bookends being signs
in Cana, plus an intervening sign in Jerusalem. To pursue this further, see my article, "The
Seventh Johannine Sign: A Study in John's Christology," *BBR* 5 (1995): 87–105, where I defend
this view in some detail. On the connection between signs in John and Isaiah, see my essay,
"John's Appropriation of Isaiah's Signs Theology: Implications for the Structure of John's Gospel,"
Themelios 43 (2018): 376–87.

the spiritual barrenness of Judaism, along with the reference to the six stone water jars for the Jewish rites of purification in verse 6.[12]

Jesus goes about his task discreetly so as not to disturb the wedding, steal the spotlight from the bride and groom, or, more importantly, reveal his messianic identity before his time. At the end of his account, John makes clear that Jesus' primary purpose was to reveal himself as the Messiah to his inner circle of disciples: "This, the first of his signs, Jesus did at Cana in Galilee, and manifested his glory. And his disciples believed in him" (2:11). This verse echoes the statement in the prologue that John and his fellow apostles "perceived [Jesus'] glory" (1:14).

Interestingly, in Greek, the "first" of Jesus' signs is literally the "head" sign (*archē*), the same word used in the phrase "in the *beginning*" in the first verse of the Gospel. So, then, this is the "beginning" of the perfect, sevenfold revelation of Jesus' messianic signs.

As noted earlier, John was concerned less with the powerful *works* of Jesus (the *dynameis*) than with his messianic *signs* (*sēmeia*). Notice how John doesn't even record the actual miracle. In fact, he refers to the master of the feast tasting "the water now become wine" in verse 9 almost in passing. In this way, John gets the ball rolling as far as Jesus' signs are concerned.

THE TEMPLE CLEARING IN JERUSALEM:
JESUS' SECOND MESSIANIC SIGN (2:13–22)

John weds (pun intended) the first sign in Galilee with the temple clearing in Jerusalem at the occasion of the Jewish Passover. Again, Jesus acts the part of the Messiah. He drives out the merchants from the temple area with messianic authority because he is zealous for the worship of God. The backstory here is that the temple courts (Grk. *hieron*) outside the actual temple building (Grk. *naos*) were

---

12. See the interesting article on this topic by Ray Clendenen, "Jesus' Blood at the Wedding in Cana?," *JETS* 63 (2020), who argues that wine is not only an emblem of end-time messianic joy but also of God's wrath, which Jesus took upon himself at the cross (cf. Jer 25:15; Rev 14:10).

the place where gentiles could worship, but merchants had set up a currency exchange business in that space in addition to selling sacrificial animals. gentile worship, therefore, was supplanted by greedy profiteering and religious hucksterism.

Like David when he faced Goliath, Jesus shows holy zeal and righteous indignation, saying, "Take these things away; do not make my Father's house a house of trade" (2:16). His words recall what he said in Luke's Gospel as a twelve-year-old—that his parents should have known he would be in his "Father's house" (Luke 2:49). At this display of spiritual zeal for the worship of God and the sacredness of the temple, the Jewish authorities—who were in charge of the temple—challenge Jesus and ask for a sign of his authority: "What sign do you show us for doing these things?" (2:18). Give us a sign!

This is an example of fine Johannine irony, as John uses the word "sign" with a double meaning. On the one hand, "sign" simply means proof of Jesus' authority. On the other hand, it means "messianic sign of Jesus," like the one he has just performed at the Cana wedding. We can see this double meaning in Jesus' response. Rather than offer them another *sign*, he proceeds to explain the *significance of the temple clearing he has just performed*. He says, "Destroy this temple, and in three days I will raise it up" (2:19). The double meaning related to the word "temple" here sets up another misunderstanding. Jesus knew his opponents would think that by "this temple" he was referring to the literal temple, but he was in fact speaking about the "temple" of his body. That is exactly the point the evangelist makes in verse 21.

Sure enough, the Jewish authorities take the bait and swallow it hook, line, and sinker, retorting, "It has taken forty-six years to build this temple, and will you raise it up in three days?" (2:20). John records no answer on Jesus' part, nor is an answer necessary. The reader understands that Jesus has just explained that the temple clearing was a sign of Jesus' messianic authority, which symbolized the resurrection of his body after three days in the grave.

Incidentally, the reference to a forty-six-year period of building this temple, as most translations render it, is most likely mistaken.

We know from historical sources that the actual restoration of the temple *building* (*naos*) was accomplished in 17 BC during the reign of Herod the Great. The restoration of the remaining temple *area* (*hieron*), however, was not completed until shortly before the Romans destroyed the temple in AD 70. So, I believe what the Jewish leaders are referring to here is not the *duration* of forty-six years of renovating the temple (or temple area) but the point in time—forty-six years *ago*—at which the renovation of the temple building had been completed. Consider this:

+ The word for "temple" here is *naos*, which refers to the temple *building*, not the temple area, which would be *hieron*.

+ The phrase "forty-six years" is in the dative, not accusative. The dative usually denotes a point in time, not duration of time, so the phrase is better rendered as a *point of time* "forty-six years ago" rather than as indicating a forty-six-year *period* ("for forty-six years") of restoring the temple.

+ The tense-form for "building" the temple is aorist, which normally refers globally to an act being performed; the progressive nature of an action is typically conveyed by the present or imperfect tense-form, neither of which is used.

Taking these points into account, verse 20 could read, in a sense, "The renovation of the temple building was completed forty-six years ago, and you will raise it up in three days?" With this phrasing, the contrast is between the long time that has passed since the renovation of the temple building was completed and the incredibly short time in which Jesus is proposing to rebuild a destroyed temple—a mere three days.

This passage helps us determine the year in which Jesus began his ministry. The temple's renovation was completed in 17 BC. Forty-six years after that brings us to AD 29, which yields a date of AD 33 for Jesus' crucifixion, assuming a three-and-a-half-year ministry.[13]

What is even more important theologically is that Jesus here presents his own crucified and resurrected body as the replacement of the Jewish temple. This is especially significant given that, when John writes his Gospel—almost certainly after the destruction of the physical temple in the year AD 70—he knows that the temple has already been destroyed.[14] So, what John is suggesting here is that anyone who was mourning the loss of the temple as a place for worship need no longer mourn. They could and should worship the risen Jesus instead!

You see this theme resurface in Jesus' conversation with the Samaritan woman, where Jesus says that true worshipers worship God in spirit and truth, regardless of the sanctuary's physical location (4:24).[15]

CONCLUSION

We've arrived at the end of our study of this portion of John's Gospel. We've explored the opening salvos of the Cana Cycle—the first (Galilean) sign at the wedding in Cana and the second (Judean) sign at the Jerusalem Passover.

I should add that John's concept of "sign" is broader than our concept of "miracle." So even though the temple clearing, unlike the turning of water at the Cana wedding, is not, technically speaking, miraculous in that it does not show Jesus overcoming any natural

---

13. For more on the date of Jesus' crucifixion, see my article, "April 3, AD 33: Why We Believe We Can Know the Exact Date Jesus Died," *First Things*, April 3, 2014, https://www. firstthings.com/web-exclusives/2014/04/ april-3-ad-33.

14. On the date and occasion of John's Gospel, see *Theology of John's Gospel and Letters*, 93–97. See also *The Cradle, the Cross, and the Crown*, 355–61.

15. To pursue this further, see the article I have written, in which I relate the composition of John's Gospel to the destruction of the temple and argue that John's Gospel was written, at least in part, to commend faith in Jesus in the aftermath of the destruction of the temple: "The Destruction of the Second Temple and the Composition of the Fourth Gospel," in *Challenging Perspectives on the Gospel of John*, WUNT 2/219, ed. John Lierman (Tübingen: Mohr-Siebeck, 2006), 69–108.

laws, it still qualifies as a Johannine sign because John's concept of "sign" encompasses both the miraculous and the prophetic.

A survey of the Old Testament concept of "sign" (Grk. *sēmeion*)[16] demonstrates that, on the one hand, there are the "signs and wonders" Moses performed at the exodus that *are* miraculous, and, on the other hand, the term *sēmeion* is applied in the Old Testament to prophetic symbolism, such as when the prophet Isaiah walks around stripped down to his undergarments for three years to signify God's judgment at the upcoming Babylonian exile (Isa 20:3). While there is nothing intrinsically miraculous about the sight of a near-naked prophet, the Septuagint (the Greek translation of the Hebrew Scriptures) still calls this a "sign" because Isaiah's act prophetically visualizes God's future judgment on his people. I believe this is exactly the sense in which John here uses the word "sign" with regard to Jesus' clearing of the temple. In prophetic style, Jesus provides a graphic demonstration of the coming judgment on the people of Israel. The physical temple would be destroyed because God condemned the corrupt worship performed there. Instead, people must repent and believe in Jesus, the temple's replacement, in order to receive eternal life.

---

16. Köstenberger, "Seventh Johannine Sign."

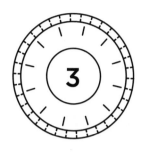

THE CANA CYCLE

PART 2

*Jesus' Conversations with Nicodemus
and the Samaritan Woman
(John 3–4)*

—

I n the previous two chapters, I argued for the apostle John being the author of John's Gospel. I spent some time examining John's prologue as it sets the stage for the rest of the Gospel. I also covered John 2, the first portion of the Cana Cycle, where John narrates Jesus' first sign, the turning of water into wine at the wedding at Cana in Galilee, and the second sign, the clearing of the temple in Jerusalem (one of Jesus' Jerusalem signs).

Now let's move on to examine the remainder of the Cana Cycle, John 3 and 4. In these chapters John features two parallel characters, Nicodemus and the Samaritan woman, and then concludes the cycle with the healing of the gentile centurion's son. In this way, John shows Jesus' mission from Jerusalem (Nicodemus) to Samaria (the Samaritan woman) to the gentiles (the ends of the earth). This shows that the early church's mission, as narrated in the book of Acts (see esp. Acts 1:8), is grounded in the mission of none other than the earthly Jesus himself.

I believe this is one of several clues that John may have read Acts (or at least been aware of its existence and basic narrative layout). Another clue lies in the two-part structure of John's Gospel: the Book of Signs (John 1–12) and the Book of Exaltation (John 13–20). In the first part, John narrates Jesus' ministry to the Jewish people, especially his seven messianic signs. In the second part, John narrates Jesus' ministry to the Twelve, the Jewish believing remnant—the new messianic community. This is where he anticipates Jesus' exaltation with the Father and the church's mission once he has been crucified, buried, and resurrected. So John sets out to accomplish in two halves of his one Gospel what Luke accomplishes in two separate but related volumes, the Gospel of Luke and the book of Acts. This is yet another possible way in which John's structure and overall approach may reflect his awareness of other New Testament writings.

INTRODUCTION: JESUS' KNOWLEDGE OF PEOPLE'S HEARTS (2:23–25)

As we begin to study John's parallel accounts of Nicodemus and the Samaritan woman in John 3 and 4, we notice that they start at 2:23, with 2:23–25 serving both as a conclusion to the temple clearing and as an introduction to the Nicodemus narrative. If you're preaching or teaching on this portion of John, I recommend you start with 2:23 and go until 3:15 or 3:21. You could either preach two sermons, one each on John 3 and John 4, or do what I'm doing here and preach or teach both together as a study in contrasts.

There are several links between 2:23–25 and 3:1 that indicate John wants us to read 2:23–25 as an introduction to the Nicodemus narrative. For instance, in 2:23, John writes that "many believed" in Jesus "when they saw the *signs* that he was doing" (emphasis added). Then, in 3:2, Nicodemus says, "no one can do these *signs* that you do unless God is with him" (emphasis added). In 2:24–25, John writes that Jesus "did not entrust himself to them," that is, the people who believed in him. Here we find a play on words in the original Greek: they "trusted" in him, but he did not "trust" in them. The reason Jesus trusted no one is that he knew what was in people's hearts and therefore needed no one to bear witness about "man" (*anthrōpos*); he already knew what was in "man" (*anthrōpos*). Then, 3:1 opens like this: "Now there was a *man* (*anthrōpos*) of the Pharisees named Nicodemus. ... This man came to Jesus by night." When we reconnect what is severed by the English chapter division, it becomes clear that Nicodemus is one of the "men" (or "people") to whom Jesus did not entrust himself because he knew what was in their hearts and saw that, despite their external expressions of faith—or even flattery—they didn't truly understand who he was.

In this way, we can see Nicodemus as representative of people who profess to be open to Jesus but lack true spiritual insight and understanding and therefore spiritual regeneration. Nicodemus further becomes a representative of all followers of Judaism who, despite all their external religious rituals and temple worship, lacked true spiritual vitality. This is reminiscent of Jeremiah's prophecy regarding a new covenant in which God would write his law onto people's hearts (Jer 31:31–34), as well as Ezekiel's vision of the valley of dry bones (Ezek 37) and his repeated predictions of future divine cleansing and renewal for God's people (e.g., Ezek 36:25–26).

THE NICODEMUS NARRATIVE (JOHN 3)

Those who understand the connection between 2:23–25 and the Nicodemus narrative in John 3 will read John 3 with a hefty grain of salt. Scholars debate whether Nicodemus' coming to Jesus by night is symbolic of him being in spiritual darkness. Personally, I think that's just when he came, but it's possible that there are negative spiritual overtones as well (that's certainly the case with the reference to Judas stepping into the night at 13:30).

OPENING PLEASANTRIES

When Nicodemus calls Jesus "rabbi" and tells him, "We know that you are a teacher come from God, for no one can do these signs that you do unless God is with him" (3:2), we shouldn't take these compliments at face value—especially when we recognize Nicodemus lived in a culture where people commonly extended the expected opening pleasantries before getting to the point of their visit.[1] We shouldn't be surprised that Jesus doesn't fall for the flattery either. Instead, he immediately cuts to the chase. He changes the topic and gets right to the heart of the matter—no small talk here—and declares, "Truly,

---

1. Peter Cotterell and Max Turner have a great study of this in their book *Linguistics and Biblical Interpretation* (Downers Grove, IL: IVP, 1989). For another biblical example, see the preamble to an address by a certain Tertullus to the Roman governor Felix in Acts 24:2–4. The same principle applies to ancient letters, which typically opened with a set of pleasantries, small talk, or well-wishes before getting to the point.

truly, I say to you, unless one is born again, he cannot see the kingdom of God" (3:3).

This is the only reference to the kingdom of God in all of John's Gospel (though Jesus speaks of his "kingdom" at his Roman trial before Pilate in 18:36). John normally eschews "kingdom of God" language and instead speaks of "eternal life."[2] For first-century Palestinian Jews, how people enter God's kingdom was a vital question, and Jesus asserts that they do so only if they have been "born again" or "born from above." The Greek word *anōthen* can have a double meaning; it can mean both "again" and "from above." For instance, the same word is used in the other Gospels to speak of the temple veil tearing "from top to bottom"—literally, "from above"—at the crucifixion (cf. Matt 27:51).

Nicodemus, lacking spiritual insight, misunderstands and thinks Jesus spoke literally of being born for a second time. Readers of the Gospel know Jesus was speaking about a birth "from above," a spiritual birth, since John already talked about this in the prologue: "But to all who did receive him, who believed in his name, he gave the right to become children of God, who were born, not of blood nor of the will of the flesh nor of the will of man, but of God" (1:12–13). It is only a small step to realize that being born "of God" is the same as being born "from above."

THE NEW BIRTH

Jesus clarifies his meaning in verse 5: "Unless one is born *of water and the Spirit*, he cannot enter the kingdom of God" (emphasis added). The phrase "born of water" could refer to natural birth or possibly water baptism, but it more likely echoes Ezekiel 36:25–27, where God says, "I will sprinkle *clean water* on you, and you shall be clean from all your uncleannesses, and from all your idols I will cleanse you. And I will give you a new heart, and a *new spirit* I will put within you. And

---

2. For a concise treatment, see Patrick Schreiner, *The Kingdom of God and the Glory of the Cross*, SSBT (Wheaton: Crossway, 2018), esp. 97–98.

I will remove the heart of stone from your flesh and give you a heart of flesh. And I will put my Spirit within you, and cause you to walk in my statutes and be careful to obey my rules" (emphasis added). Water, therefore, is a metaphor for spiritual cleansing, accompanied by God giving people "a new heart, and a new spirit."

Many translations, including the ESV (cited above), capitalize "Spirit" in verse 5, indicating that they think Jesus spoke to Nicodemus about a new birth by the Holy Spirit. I think it is more likely that Jesus was merely talking about a spiritual birth (lowercase "s"). Consider the next few verses, where he says, "That which is born of the flesh is flesh, and that which is born of the Spirit is spirit. ... The wind [Grk. *pneuma*, the same word as for "spirit"] blows where it wishes, and you hear its sound, but you do not know where it comes from or where it goes. So it is with everyone who is born of the Spirit" (3:6–8). He refers to experiencing a spiritual rather than mere natural birth. Again, most translations capitalize "Spirit" here, but I believe it is more likely that Jesus is contrasting a natural and a spiritual birth by way of the "flesh/spirit" (*sarx/pneuma*) contrast rather than specifying the agent of the new birth as the Holy Spirit. In any case, this would have been all but unintelligible for Jesus' original conversation partner, Nicodemus, who simply replies, incredulously, "How can these things be?" (3:9). That said, even in the above-cited passage from Ezekiel, the prophet speaks both of a "new spirit" and "my [God's] Spirit," so that both may be in view.

Notice how Nicodemus' comments get shorter and shorter the deeper he gets into the conversation (cf. 3:2, 4, 9). This is in contrast to the Samaritan woman in the next chapter, whose responses get longer and longer. In fact, this is the last we hear Nicodemus speak in this story; he, the teacher of Israel, has been reduced to silence by Jesus (though the Fourth Evangelist refers to him at two later occasions, a Sanhedrin meeting and Jesus' burial; 7:50–51; 19:39).

Jesus chides Nicodemus for his lack of spiritual understanding, saying, "Are you the teacher of Israel and yet you do not understand these things?" (3:10). In other words, Jesus implies that Nicodemus should have known about a spiritual birth from passages in Ezekiel or Jeremiah. And if the "teacher of Israel" doesn't know such vital matters, what does that tell you about the rest of the followers of Judaism?

In the remainder of his speech, Jesus broadens the scope of reference and shifts from the singular to the plural. In this way, he mimics Nicodemus' own language at the beginning when he told Jesus, "We know that you are a teacher come from God" (3:2, emphasis added). Repeating Nicodemus' diction, Jesus says, "Truly, truly, I say to you, we speak of what we know, and bear witness to what we have seen, but you [plural, referring to the people] do not receive our testimony" (3:11, emphasis added). Most likely, Jesus' plural "we" includes previous witnesses such as the prophets or perhaps current witnesses such as his disciples.[3]

THE GOSPEL OF THE CROSS

Jesus goes on to say, "If I have told you earthly things and you do not believe, how can you believe if I tell you heavenly things?" (3:12). The teaching about a new birth is not only elementary but earthly, while the teaching about Jesus' true heavenly origin and upcoming cross-work is more advanced and heavenly. At this, Jesus identifies himself as the Son of Man who descended *from* heaven and will return *to* heaven. He also speaks of his future "lifting up" (echoing the third Servant Song in Isaiah, cf. Isa 52:13), comparing it to Moses lifting up the serpent in the wilderness (John 3:13–14).

You may be familiar with the account to which Jesus refers. Numbers 21:4–9 recounts how, during Israel's wilderness wanderings following the exodus, the people complained that God brought them out of Egypt only to die in the wilderness. God consequently sent fiery serpents that (ironically) bit and killed many people. When the people repented and Moses interceded for them, God provided a rather peculiar means of deliverance. He told Moses to lift up a bronze

---

3. See Allan Chapple, "Jesus and the Witnesses (John 3:11)," *JETS* 63 (2020), who argues that the witnesses are the OT prophets, John the Baptist, and culminating in Jesus himself.

serpent (note that in this case, a serpent is a positive image, conveying *deliverance* from death rather than being the *cause* of death as in the garden of Eden), and any Israelite who looked at it and believed would be spared. In the same way, Jesus says, God would lift *him* up, so that everyone who would look at *him* in faith would receive eternal, spiritual life.[4] The alert reader will detect in this a veiled reference to Jesus' crucifixion.

Jesus was preaching the gospel to Nicodemus! The entire conversation with the teacher of Israel thus becomes a penetrating and highly instructive case study of how to share the gospel with nominal Christians, religious people who think they're already saved when they're really not. Ask them if they know about their need for spiritual rebirth and proclaim to them that they can be born again if they believe in the crucified and risen Jesus. I've had conversations like this with my own mother, father, and sister, all of whom come from a Roman Catholic background where traditions sometimes obstruct a true spiritual understanding and the central place of the gospel, just like they did in Nicodemus' day.

JESUS' USE OF TYPOLOGY

Jesus used typology to preach the gospel to Nicodemus. Typology is a device by which one establishes a historical, "typical" connection between God's acts in earlier times (the "type") and his later acts in salvation history (the "antitype"). Notice I said "historical." In the present case, the original instance (the "type") took place in the days of the exodus, while the corresponding event (the "antitype") was to take place in the near future, at the crucifixion. The pattern of correspondence was between an original "lifting up" of an object (the bronze serpent) and people's looking at it in faith, and a later "lifting up" of another object (Jesus) and people's looking at him in faith.

---

4. See the two later "lifted up sayings" in 8:28 and 12:32–34, esp. v. 33—"He said this to show by what kind of death he was going to die"—which gradually reveal that by "lifting up" the evangelist is referring to Jesus' death on the cross.

So, there is a historical pattern of correspondence based on the dual notion that history unfolds progressively along certain lines and that God acts consistently in history. What is more, not only is there a typical, historical pattern, but the pattern is shown to be of an *escalating* nature. In other words, the pattern does not merely repeat itself, but there is a further development from type to antitype. In the present case, the development is from the preservation of *physical* life to the reception of *spiritual*, eternal life. And there is also a massive further escalation from Moses lifting up the bronze serpent to God's only Son, the Lord Jesus Christ, being lifted up on a Roman cross as God's lamb who gave his life for the sins of the world (cf. 1:29, 36).

Jesus here provides us with a textbook example of typology in grounding his future cross-death in a scriptural antecedent of which Nicodemus would have been well aware. What is more, Jesus didn't merely show off his ability to unearth typology; rather, he genuinely sought to illustrate the spiritual dynamic underlying the crucifixion with a biblical example in order to enhance its plausibility and scriptural undergirding. Earlier in the conversation he had similarly tried to explain the nature of the spiritual birth by using an illustration from nature, the mysterious character of the wind (3:6–8).

TRANSITION TO EVANGELIST'S COMMENTARY

Verse 15 seems to be transitional, moving from Jesus' words to the evangelist's commentary, as here we find Johannine language: "that whoever believes in him may have eternal life" (cf. 3:16: "that whoever believes in him should ... have eternal life"). Many red-letter editions of our Bibles show verses 16–21 in red, indicating they are Jesus' words; I believe, however, that these verses should not be put in red letters as they are almost certainly the evangelist's commentary. This would in no way detract from the incredible declaration made in the beloved verse John 3:16: "For God so loved the world, that he gave his only Son, that whoever believes in him should not perish but have eternal life."

We don't have time here to unpack this verse completely. I've heard entire sermons preached on this verse, discussing it word by word. But one aspect of this verse that I will address is something I hadn't noticed until recently: that for Nicodemus, the notion that God loves the entire world would have been anything but self-evident. First-century Jews commonly believed that God only loved Israel while reserving the gentiles for judgment. We see this belief, for example, in the War Scroll at Qumran or Jesus' statement in the Sermon on the Mount, "You have heard that it was said, 'You shall love your neighbor and hate your enemy.' But I say to you, Love your enemies and pray for those who persecute you" (Matt 5:43–44).[5] This, then, is another aspect of escalation in Jesus' typology. While in the first instance, it was *Israelites* whose lives were preserved during the exodus, Jesus' cross-death would be an expression of God's love for the *entire world*, and, as a result, *whoever* believed in Jesus would receive eternal life.

The reference to Jesus as God's "one and only Son" echoes the dual reference to Jesus as the "one and only Son" in John's prologue (1:14, 18; Grk. *monogenēs*; see also 3:18). This is another important indication that here we have moved from Jesus' speech (who just called himself, twice, the "Son of Man," 3:13, 14) to the evangelist's. Both references to Jesus as God's "one and only Son" and to God "giving" (rather than "sending") his Son also connect John's statement with the Abraham narrative in Genesis 22, the famous near-sacrifice of Isaac. The Septuagint refers to Isaac as Abraham's "one and only son" because he, not Ishmael, was the son God had promised to Abraham (Gen 22:2: "Take your son, *your only son* Isaac, whom you love," emphasis added).

So we see in this entire passage several vital connections between Jesus and the cross, on the one hand, and the Old Testament, on the other: references to Abraham and Isaac, and Moses and the exodus;

---

5. See my article "Lifting Up the Son of Man and God's Love for the World: John 3:16 in Its Historical, Literary, and Theological Contexts," in *Understanding the Times: New Testament Studies in the 21st Century: Essays in Honor of D. A. Carson on the Occasion of His 65th Birthday*, ed. Andreas J. Köstenberger and Robert W. Yarbrough (Wheaton: Crossway, 2011), 141–59.

an important allusion to Isaiah (the Servant being "lifted up"); and another allusion to Ezekiel's prophecy of the new birth. This incredibly impressive array of Old Testament passages show that Jesus' mission had numerous points of contact with God's previous interactions with his people in Israel's history. The Fourth Evangelist makes it clear that Jesus' coming serves as the culmination of God's redemptive and revelatory purposes. So much for "unhitching" the New Testament from the Old! We can see that Jesus and John here do the exact opposite. They show that the gospel is grounded in Old Testament narrative, typology, and prophecy and thus render the gospel more intelligible, compellingly, and skillfully illumining its deeper meaning.

THE REST OF CHAPTER 3

Following his commentary in verses 16–21, John narrates Jesus' departure from Jerusalem and journey to the Judean countryside (3:22). He then once again shines the spotlight on John the Baptist. While he previously cast him primarily as one of the many witnesses to Jesus (cf. 1:6–8, 15, 19–37), he now presents him in a different metaphor as the "friend of the bridegroom" who happily facilitates the wedding of bride and groom (3:29). Just like the best man in a wedding, he must fade into the background so as not to steal the spotlight from the groom.

JESUS AND THE SAMARITAN WOMAN (JOHN 4)

The interface between Jesus' forerunner, John the Baptist, and Jesus becomes the subject of the transitional statement in 4:1: "Now when Jesus learned that the Pharisees had heard that Jesus was making and baptizing more disciples than John ..." The narrative makes it clear that Jesus is not embroiled in any competition or rivalry with John—competing over who could perform more baptisms than the other. Rather, Jesus leaves Judea (4:3; cf. 3:22) and travels to Galilee by way of Samaria (4:3–4).

Interestingly, verse 4 asserts that Jesus "had to" (Grk. *dei*) pass through Samaria. In fact, he didn't *have* to pass through Samaria. Many

Jews in that day took a longer route in order to *avoid* passing through Samaria. Apparently here the evangelist stresses *divine necessity*: Jesus "had to" pass through Samaria because this was part of God's plan. In this passage, as before, we also find interesting salvation-historical connections, this time with Jacob's well and Joseph's field in verses 5 and 6.[6]

A STUDY IN CONTRASTS

While the story of Jesus' encounter with the Samaritan woman is unique in and of itself, John deliberately juxtaposes this account with Jesus' interchange with Nicodemus in order to compare and contrast their respective responses. Consider the following contrasts:

FIG. 4: A STUDY IN CONTRASTS: NICODEMUS AND THE SAMARITAN WOMAN (JOHN 3–4)

he was a man; she was a woman

he was a Jew; she a Samaritan, from a hated, hybrid race

he was the "teacher of Israel"; she remains unnamed

he was a member of the Sanhedrin; she was a nobody

he knew the Scriptures; she was mired in folklore and tradition

he was the epitome of morality; she was an immoral woman

he comes by night; she comes in broad daylight at noon

Humanly speaking, Nicodemus towers over the Samaritan in every respect. Yet John shows a dramatic reversal when it comes to spiritual understanding. In fact, we see a remarkable progression of the woman's understanding of Jesus. She first calls him "a Jew" (4:9). When, in a striking display of supernatural knowledge, he tells her about her previous relationships, she calls him "a prophet" (4:19). Then, when he identifies himself to her plainly as the Messiah (which Jesus rarely

---

6. See the previous allusion to Jacob's ladder at 1:51 above.

did in any of the other Gospels; cf. the "messianic secret" motif), she concludes that he likely is "the Christ" (4:29).

What is more, while Nicodemus fades silently into the night, Jesus having reduced him to silence, the woman bears eloquent witness to her fellow Samaritans in broad daylight, inviting them to come meet Jesus and see this remarkable prophet and likely Messiah for themselves. The teacher of Israel is reduced to silence and exposed for his lack of spiritual understanding while the Samaritan woman turns into an evangelist. Quite a contrast!

This is in keeping with Jesus' pattern of reversal elsewhere, including instances where Samaritans emerge as the heroes of the story, such as the parable of the good Samaritan (Luke 10:25–37) or the story of the ten healed lepers (Luke 17:11–19). John's convicting message for his original readers—and for all of us today—is that spiritual receptivity will often be found in those who lack status, power, and prestige in this world. You see this also in Paul's ministry: in Athens, where he is debating the philosophers, only a handful of people believe (Acts 17:16–34); in contrast, in some of the less highbrow places he visits, there is a much larger response and churches are established. As Paul wrote to the Corinthians,

> For consider your calling, brothers: not many of you were wise according to worldly standards, not many were powerful, not many were of noble birth. But God chose what is foolish in the world to shame the wise; God chose what is weak in the world to shame the strong; God chose what is low and despised in the world, even things that are not, to bring to nothing things that are, so that no human being might boast in the presence of God. (1 Cor 1:26–29)

John tells us that "many Samaritans from that town believed in him because of the woman's testimony" (4:39); and then, "many more believed because of his word" (4:41).

In this account, we see Jesus breaking just about every social taboo upheld by first-century Jewish rabbis and Scripture-literate males.

Most egregiously, he talks to a woman alone in public—and not just any woman but an immoral one from a hated, hybrid, impure race. And he doesn't just talk to her briefly—he engages her in extended conversation! He is even willing to take a cup of water from her, even though Jews had "no dealings" with Samaritans and didn't associate with them, which included not touching any of their vessels or other belongings (4:9). He even accepts the Samaritans' invitation to stay with them for two days (4:40). No wonder his disciples "marveled that he was talking with a woman" (4:27)!

In the introductory chapter, I mentioned the hermeneutical triad of history, literature, and theology. This is a great example of how knowing historical-cultural background can be really helpful in getting the full sense of a passage.

THE HEALING OF THE
CENTURION'S SON (4:46–54)

The Cana Cycle concludes with another of Jesus' signs, the healing of the gentile centurion's son (4:46–54). Most of Jesus' signs involve a numerical detail: the large amount of wine Jesus produced at the Cana wedding, the forty-six years vs. three days at the temple clearing, the healing of the man who had been lame for thirty-eight years, the feeding of the five thousand, the raising of Lazarus four days after he died. This story is no exception. Here the numerical detail is the exact time—one o'clock in the afternoon—when Jesus healed the centurion's son from a long distance.

CONCLUSION

As we conclude our study of the Cana Cycle (John 2–4), we see that this portion of Scripture provides a fascinating case study in both *Johannine* theology and *mission* theology.[7] With regard to *Johannine*

---

7. I wrote my doctoral dissertation on the mission theme in John's Gospel, on John 20:21, "As the Father sent me, so I am sending you": *The Missions of Jesus and the Disciples according to the Fourth Gospel* (Grand Rapids: Eerdmans, 1998). See also the chapter on John's trinitarian

theology, we see here three of Jesus' seven messianic signs selected for inclusion in this Gospel. All of these are public acts of Jesus designed to lead people to faith in him as Messiah and Son of God.

With regard to *mission* theology, we see Jesus provide textbook examples of engaging people from various backgrounds—religious and non-religious, moral and immoral, powerful and powerless. They are male and female, Jew and gentile, high status and low status. In this way, the Cana Cycle serves as a powerful narrative demonstration of the veracity of Paul's words in Galatians 3:28: "There is neither Jew nor Greek, there is neither slave nor free, there is no male and female, for you are all one in Christ Jesus."

With this, we've come to the end of the Cana Cycle. In the next chapter, we will embark on our next journey. This time, our journey will take us not from Cana and back to Cana. Rather, we will shadow Jesus and his followers as they attend various Jewish festivals, both in the Judean south (Jerusalem) and the Galilean north. What will happen there? You'll have to read the next few chapters to find out.

---

mission theology in *Father, Son and Spirit: The Trinity and John's Gospel,* NSBT 24 (Downers Grove, IL: IVP, 2008), a volume I co-authored with Scott R. Swain.

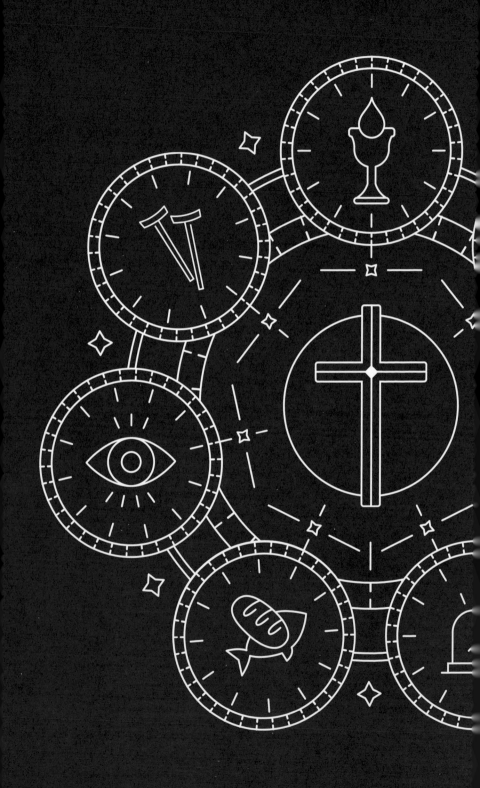

FESTIVAL CYCLE

(JOHN 5-10)

4

THE FESTIVAL CYCLE

PART 1

The Healing of the Lame Man
(John 5)

———

THE FESTIVAL CYCLE

PART 1

The Healing of the Lame Man
(John 5)

I n the first three chapters we made a promising start by discussing the authorship of John's Gospel, which is exceedingly important in interpreting the book in keeping with its authorial intent and original historical setting. We also studied John's prologue or introduction (John 1:1–18) in some depth and then moved on to take a closer look at the Cana Cycle (John 2–4).

The designation Cana Cycle, as mentioned, derives from the fact that this literary unit of John's Gospel starts and ends with signs Jesus performed in the small village of Cana in the Galilean north. John deliberately structured his presentation of the early stages of Jesus' public work in the form of a ministry circuit beginning and ending in Cana, a rather obscure Galilean town not even mentioned in any of the other Gospels. John indicated this by referring to Jesus' first and second signs in Cana in John 2:11 and 4:54, respectively.

In between these two Cana signs, we saw Jesus clear the temple (one of his Jerusalem signs; cf. 2:23; 3:2) and go on mission from Jerusalem (2:13–3:21) and Judea (3:22) to Samaria (4:1–45) and the gentiles (4:46–54), where he ministered first to Nicodemus, the Jewish rabbi, then to an unnamed Samaritan woman, and finally to a gentile official. In this way, we saw how the early church's mission—which by the time John wrote his Gospel would already have been in full swing—was grounded in the mission of Jesus himself.

All of this was shown to serve John's overarching purpose: to narrate selected messianic signs of Jesus in order to elicit faith in him among his readers and others with whom they might come in contact (20:30–31).

As to these signs, we saw that the Cana Cycle featured three messianic signs of Jesus, exhibiting an oscillating geographical movement from Galilee to Jerusalem and back to Galilee, each in their own unique way shining the spotlight on Jesus and his messianic identity and mission. We also saw that Jesus' actions and teachings met with a variety of responses on a spectrum from faith to unbelief, which the Fourth Evangelist sought to highlight in the form of representative characters such as Nicodemus, the Samaritan woman, or the gentile official.[1]

In this and the next two chapters, we'll build on our previous study by covering the next major unit in John's Gospel, the so-called "Festival Cycle" (John 5–10). John was a master storyteller who structured his Gospel deliberately.[2] What is more, as we see in his purpose statement and in the conclusion to the entire Gospel, he was highly selective in what he chose to include. In his purpose statement, he writes, "Now Jesus did many other signs in the presence of the disciples, which are not written in this book; but these are written so that you may believe that Jesus is the Christ, the Son of God, and that by believing you may have life in his name" (20:30–31). He closes the Gospel with the words, "Now there are also many other things that Jesus did. Were every one of them to be written, I suppose that the world itself could not contain the books that would be written" (21:25).

INTRODUCTORY QUESTIONS

Before we take an in-depth look at the healing of the lame man in John 5, let's discuss a few broader questions: Why does John select these particular signs? Why do scholars believe that John 5–10 is a literary unit, why is this unit commonly called the Festival Cycle, and how does John 5–10 connect with what precedes and follows this unit?

---

1. At times scholars who don't believe the apostle John wrote the Gospel use the expression "Fourth Evangelist." I, on the other hand, am a strong advocate of Johannine authorship. When I use the term "Fourth Evangelist," I do so primarily to avoid confusion with John the Baptist and at times also for stylistic variation.

2. See, e.g., Mark W. Stibbe, *John as Storyteller: Narrative Criticism and the Fourth Gospel* (Cambridge: Cambridge University Press, 1992).

WHY THESE SIGNS?

John acknowledges that Jesus performed "many other signs" and did "many other things." Why, then, did John select these particular signs and activities from among all the material at his disposal, whether written, oral, or eyewitness memory?[3] As I will seek to demonstrate below, John's selection of material for inclusion in his Gospel was guided by at least three criteria: (1) Whether material was already included in one or several of the other Gospels (of the seven signs featured in John, only one is found in the other Gospels, the feeding of the five thousand; John also records another temple clearing and another healing of an official's son than those recounted in the Synoptics). (2) Whether a messianic sign of Jesus was particularly striking and memorable (almost always connected with large or unusual numbers). (3) Whether a given action or teaching of Jesus could be used to buttress the claim that Jesus was the Christ and Son of God and thus lead his readers to believe in him.

MATERIAL NOT ALREADY INCLUDED
IN THE OTHER GOSPELS

One important criterion in John's selection was *material not featured in the Synoptic Gospels*, which had already been written when John composed his narrative—Matthew, Mark, and Luke.

In many ways, when we read John's Gospel, we get the impression that John aimed to complement and supplement—though not replace—the other Gospels.[4] In other words, he tried not to repeat

---

3. James D. G. Dunn, *Jesus Remembered*, Christianity in the Making 1 (Grand Rapids: Eerdmans, 2003), unfortunately claims that John invented some of the material he features in his Gospel, such as large swaths of Jesus' Roman trial before Pilate. In this he is representative of much historical-critical scholarship that marginalizes John due to his alleged lack of concern for historicity. Richard Bauckham, *Jesus and the Eyewitnesses: The Gospels as Eyewitness Testimony*, 2nd ed. (Grand Rapids: Eerdmans, 2016), takes the character of the Gospels as eyewitness testimony much more seriously, but even he denies Matthean and Johannine authorship. For a critique of Bauckham, see Andreas J. Köstenberger, *A Theology of John's Gospel and Letters: The Word, the Christ, the Son of God*, BTNT (Grand Rapids: Zondervan, 2009), 75–79.

4. The relationship between John and the Synoptics is subject to considerable scholarly debate, which we cannot fully address here; though see Köstenberger, *Theology of John's Gospel*

material already found there, or at least attempted to find creative ways to deepen his readers' understanding of that material. Among the unique characters in John's Gospel are Nicodemus and the Samaritan woman, the lame man, the man born blind—who uttered the famous words, "One thing I do know, that though I was blind, now I see" (9:25)—and Lazarus, whom Jesus raised from the dead.

FIG. 5: MAJOR SELECTED CHARACTERS FEATURED
EXCLUSIVELY IN JOHN'S GOSPEL

Passage	Character	Significance
John 3	Nicodemus	Teacher of Israel, lacks regeneration
John 4	Samaritan woman	Evangelizes fellow villagers
John 5	Lame man	Healed by Jesus, intransigent
John 9	Man born blind	Eyes opened, worships Jesus
John 11	Lazarus	Raised from the dead by Jesus

Some noteworthy teachings of Jesus unique to John's Gospel are several extended discourses such as the Bread of Life Discourse (John 6), the Good Shepherd Discourse (John 10), and the Discourse of the Vine and the Branches (John 15), which in turn is part of the famous Farewell Discourse (John 13–17). This final body of teaching (also called the Upper Room Discourse) provides a unique and fascinating glimpse into Jesus' final hours with his followers unparalleled in any of the Synoptics.

and Letters, 553–63; and more fully Köstenberger, "John's Transposition Theology: Retelling the Story of Jesus in a Different Key," in Earliest Christian History: History, Literature, and Theology. Essays from the Tyndale Fellowship in Honor of Martin Hengel, ed. Michael F. Bird and Jason Maston, WUNT 2/320 (Tübingen: Mohr/Siebeck, 2012), 191–226. See also the comments below.

FIG. 6: MAJOR SELECTED DISCOURSES FEATURED
UNIQUELY IN JOHN'S GOSPEL

Passage	Discourse
John 6	Bread of Life Discourse
John 10	Good Shepherd Discourse
John 13–17	Farewell Discourse, including the Vine and the Branches

PARTICULARLY STRIKING SIGNS

A second demonstrable criterion for John's inclusion of material in his Gospel was his avowed *purpose*: to present selected (and particularly striking) messianic signs of Jesus so that his readers may believe that Jesus is the Christ, the Son of God—or, perhaps better, that the Christ, the Son of God, is Jesus (20:30–31).[5]

John selected seven signs of Jesus, including the temple clearing.[6] But why these particular signs? What virtually all the signs have in common is that they are particularly striking manifestations of Jesus' messianic mission and often involve significant numbers:

1. Jesus turns *120–150 gallons* of water into wine (2:1–12).

2. He promises to raise the temple of his body in *three days* while the temple had been built *forty-six years* ago (2:13–22).

3. He healed a man long-distance at *1 o'clock* in the afternoon (or, as it says in the original Greek, at the "seventh hour"; Jews started counting the hours of the day with sunrise at around 6 o'clock in the morning; 4:46–54).

---

5. See D. A. Carson, "The Purpose of the Fourth Gospel: Jn 20:31 Reconsidered," *JBL* 106 (1987): 639–51.

6. Andreas J. Köstenberger, "The Seventh Johannine Sign: A Study of John's Christology," *BBR* 5 (1995): 87–103.

4. He healed a man who had been crippled for *thirty-eight years* (5:1–15).

5. He fed *five thousand men* plus women and children (6:1–15; thus the "feeding of the five thousand" was more likely the "feeding of the twenty thousand").

6. He healed a man born blind (no numbers here; chap. 9).

7. He raised a man, Lazarus, who had been dead in the tomb for *four days* (11:1–44).

In this way, John highlights particularly striking signs of Jesus and includes information that eyewitnesses would have typically remembered, whether specific numbers or other minor yet important details. For instance, he records that there was "much grass" in the place where Jesus fed the five thousand (6:10) or that the fragrance of the perfume Mary poured out at the anointing filled the entire house (12:3).

FIG. 7: NUMBERS RELATED TO STRIKING
SIGNS OF JESUS IN THE BOOK OF SIGNS

Passage	Sign	Number(s)
2:1–12	Turning water into wine	120–150 gallons
2:13–22	Clearing the temple	forty-six years vs. three days
4:46–54	Healing the official's son	seventh hour (i.e., 1 p.m.)
5:1–15	Healing the lame man	thirty-eight years
6:1–15	Feeding the multitude	five thousand men (plus women and children)
9:1–41	Healing the man born blind	blind from birth
11:1–44	Raising Lazarus	four days

PROOF THAT JESUS IS THE CHRIST AND SON OF GOD

In keeping with his purpose, then, John selected material that underscored the singular and central claim in his Gospel: that *Jesus was the Messiah and Son of God*. He included material that he believed was suited to lead his readers to put their trust in Jesus. This is borne out by the fact that the verb "to believe" (Grk. *pisteuō*) is found almost one hundred times in the Gospel and that many Gospel characters serve as figures representing either a trusting or unbelieving response toward Jesus. In our study of John 3–4, we saw that Nicodemus, the Jewish rabbi, represented the unbelieving response while the Samaritan woman represented the believing response.

We'll see that in the Festival Cycle (John 5–10), John includes a similar study of comparisons and contrasts between the lame man in John 5 and the man born blind in John 9. In addition, Jesus' signs are often linked with either a major discourse or an "I am saying" of Jesus, or both. In John 6, for example, Jesus performs the sign of feeding the five thousand; proclaims that he is the Bread of Life (an "I am saying"; 6:35, 48); and delivers the so-called Bread of Life Discourse (6:32–58).

WHY CONSIDER JOHN 5–10 A LITERARY UNIT?

Let's now turn to a closer study of the Festival Cycle in John 5–10. John 2–4 is relatively free of major controversy (the temple clearing being an exception), as the Cana Cycle depicts the early stages of Jesus' ministry. All of this changes now in John 5, and the conflict continues to build in the chapters that follow.

A literary *inclusio* binds John 5 and 10 together in a concerted focus on Jesus' claim to deity and his opponents' attempts to stone him on account of perceived blasphemy. In John 5:18, toward the beginning of the Festival Cycle, the evangelist tells us, "This was why the Jews were seeking all the more to kill him [Jesus], because not only was he breaking the Sabbath, but he was even calling God his own Father, *making himself equal to God*" (emphasis added). Then, toward the end of the Festival Cycle, John narrates Jesus' claim, "I and the Father are one." At once, "the Jews picked up stones again to stone him."

When Jesus asked them for which of his "many good works" they were trying to stone him, they replied, "It is not for a good work that we are going to stone you but for blasphemy, because you, being a man, *make yourself God*" (10:30–33, emphasis added). All of this, in turn, is building up toward the eventual climax in the Gospel: Jesus' Roman trial, where the Jewish leaders tell Pilate, "We have a law, and according to that law he ought to die because *he has made himself the Son of God*" (19:7, emphasis added). So the references to Jesus' alleged blasphemy frame the entire Festival Cycle in John 5–10.

FIG. 8: THE LITERARY *INCLUSIO* FRAMING
THE FESTIVAL CYCLE (JOHN 5–10)

Passage	Escalating Conflict: References to Jesus' Perceived Blasphemy
5:18	"This was why the Jews were seeking all the more to kill him, because not only was he breaking the Sabbath, but he was even calling God his own Father, *making himself equal with God*" (emphasis added).
10:31–33	"The Jews picked up stones to stone him. ... 'It is not for a good work that we are going to stone you but for blasphemy, because you, being a man, *make yourself God*'" (emphasis added).

On a structural level, we can detect an even more all-encompassing *inclusio* that connects the material between 1:19 and 10:42. John 1:19, following immediately after the prologue, starts out like this: "And this is the testimony of John." In the chapters that follow, John is identified as a witness to Jesus (1:19–36; cf. 1:6–8, 15), the friend of the bridegroom (3:29), and a lamp that shone for a while (5:35). The last of these references—the description of John as a lamp that shone for a while—is found in John 5. Mirroring this reference, we find in John 10, at the end of the Festival Cycle, a rather surprising final reference to John the Baptist. We read, "He [Jesus] went away again across the Jordan to the place where John had been baptizing at first, and there he remained. And many came to him. And they said, 'John did no sign, but everything that John said about this man was true.' And many believed in him there" (10:40–42).

FIG. 9: THE LITERARY *INCLUSIO* FRAMING JOHN 1:19–10:42

Passage	Opening and Closing References to John the Baptist
1:19, 28	"And this is the testimony of John. ... These things took place in Bethany across the Jordan, where John was baptizing."
10:40–42	"He went away again across the Jordan to the place where John had been baptizing at first, and there he remained. ... And they said, 'John did no sign, but everything that John said about this man was true.' And many believed in him there."

Why does John include this final reference to John the Baptist? As early as at 3:24, the evangelist told his readers in an aside, "For John had not yet been put in prison."[7] For all practical purposes, John the Baptist has not been a character in the Johannine narrative since the end of chapter 3, where he announced, "He must increase, but I must decrease" (3:30). This is certainly true literally and literarily, as far as the Johannine narrative is concerned. References to the Baptist have dramatically decreased ever since his early witness to Jesus.

Why, then, mention John one more time as late as at the end of the Festival Cycle in John 10, close to the end of Jesus' mission and just prior to the raising of Lazarus, Jesus' final messianic sign recorded in John's Gospel? The answer, I believe, lies in the fact that the Fourth Evangelist wants to signal to his readers that John 5–10 (and on a larger scale John 1:19–10:42) constitutes a coherent literary unit, what

---

7. On the Johannine asides, see my *Theology of John's Gospel and Letters*, 135–41.

scholars have called the Johannine Festival Cycle. In this way, both major ministry cycles and literary units in the first ten chapters of John's Gospel are bracketed by *inclusios*: the Cana Cycle by references to Jesus' signs in Cana at 2:11 and 4:54, and the Festival Cycle by references to Jewish opposition to Jesus' claim to deity in 5:18 and 10:30–33 and to the witness of John the Baptist in 1:19 and 10:40–42.

WHY CALL THIS UNIT THE FESTIVAL CYCLE?

Why has John 5–10 earned the label Festival Cycle? References to Jewish festivals are not unique to John 5–10. In fact, in the Cana Cycle, Jesus attends a Passover festival in Jerusalem (2:13, 23). What is unique, though, is that festivals serve as a continual structural marker in the Festival Cycle.

+ John 5 finds Jesus at an unnamed festival in Jerusalem

+ John 6 shows him at Passover in Galilee

+ John 7–8 feature Jesus at the Feast of Tabernacles or Booths in Jerusalem; and

+ John 10 shows Jesus at the Feast of Dedication or Hanukkah, again in Jerusalem.

John presents Jesus as the fulfillment of the symbolism inherent in these various festivals, as embodying in his very own person the essence to which each of these festivals pointed. Jesus was infinitely greater than the entire Jewish festival calendar, and in him all these various festivals found their multifaceted messianic fulfillment. This, in addition to Jesus' messianic signs, was yet another compelling reason to call people to believe in Jesus as the Messiah and Son of God.

We've explored the question as to why the Fourth Evangelist chose to include the particular teachings and events in Jesus' life that he features in his Gospel. We've seen how John carefully structured John 5–10 around Jesus' attendance of and pronouncements at a series of Jewish festivals. Since John proceeds chronologically (albeit selectively), we can see just how selective he is by taking a closer look at the festivals Jesus is shown to attend. If the first feast in the Festival Cycle, though unnamed in John's Gospel, is Tabernacles (a feast celebrated in September or October every year), as may be indicated by some textual variants and extrabiblical evidence, John 5 would record events taking place in the fall.[8] John 6 takes place at Passover, which was celebrated in the spring. Then, John 7 opens with another Tabernacles festival; thus, an entire year has passed since John 5 (assuming that the reference in 5:1 is to Tabernacles). Finally, the Feast of Dedication took place in the winter (10:22). Thus, the entire Festival Cycle spans a little over a year in Jesus' three-and-a-half-year ministry.

FIG. 10: JEWISH FESTIVALS IN THE JOHANNINE FESTIVAL CYCLE (JOHN 5–10)

Passage	Festival	Time Celebrated
5:1	"A feast of the Jews" (Tabernacles?)	Fall
6:3	Passover	Spring
7:1	Tabernacles (or Booths)	Fall
10:22	Dedication (Hanukkah)	Winter

JESUS' HEALING OF THE LAME MAN (JOHN 5)

Now that we've been oriented to this second major cycle in John's Gospel, let's turn to the first literary unit in the Festival Cycle, Jesus' healing of the lame man in John 5.

---

8. The earliest papyri ($\mathfrak{P}^{66, 75}$) and codices (A, B) omit the definite article and simply have, "After this there was *a feast* of the Jews," which makes this the probable original reading. Yet some manuscripts (such as Sinaiticus [א]) include the definite article ("After this there was 'the' feast of the Jews," which most likely would have referred to Tabernacles). What is more, at least one manuscript actually has "Tabernacles" (131), which shows that some later scribes interpreted the reference as being to Tabernacles. See the discussion in Bruce M. Metzger, *A Textual Commentary on the Greek New Testament*, 2nd ed. (New York: United Bible Societies, 1994), 178.

THE SETTING (5:1–3)

In the introduction to this account, John masterfully sets the stage for the first messianic sign of Jesus narrated in the Festival Cycle. He tells us:

1. that there was a Jewish festival (5:1)

2. that Jesus went up to Jerusalem, the Jewish capital (5:1); and

3. that there was in Jerusalem by the Sheep Gate a pool called Bethesda, which had five roofed colonnades (5:2).[9] This area, John tells us, was a common gathering place for a large number of invalids, whether blind, lame, or paralyzed (5:1–3).

After this, a verse is missing in most of our English Bibles. Verse 4, which is found only in a few later manuscripts, inserts that the invalids were "waiting for the moving of the water, for an angel of the Lord went down at certain seasons into the pool and stirred the water; whoever stepped in first after the stirring of the water was healed of whatever disease he had." This is the type of material that was characteristic of so-called apocryphal or spurious (i.e., inauthentic) gospels, which contained legendary material and reflected popular superstitions. Therefore, the verse is rightly omitted from the standard Greek text and most English versions.[10]

---

9. On the many ways in which recent archeological finds have buttressed the historicity of John's Gospel and aided our understanding of the historical setting of John's Gospel, see Urban C. von Wahlde, "Archaeology and John's Gospel," in *Jesus and Archaeology*, ed. James H. Charlesworth (Grand Rapids: Eerdmans, 2006), 523–86. On the pool of Bethesda specifically, see pp. 560–66. Von Wahlde concludes, "The discovery of the pools proved beyond a doubt that the description of this pool was not the creation of the Evangelist but reflected accurate and detailed knowledge of Jerusalem" (566).

10. Verse 4 is not found in the earliest papyrus MSS, $\mathfrak{P}^{66}$ and $\mathfrak{P}^{75}$. It is also absent from the earliest codices, Sinaiticus ($\aleph$) and Vaticanus (B).

THE HEALING (5:5–9A)

After this, the narrative focuses on one such invalid, a man who had been in this condition for thirty-eight years. This must have seemed like an eternity for the man to be languishing without a realistic chance of being healed. One of the reasons John may have chosen to include this sign is that there was virtually no way this miracle could have been staged. The man had been lying there for thirty-eight years, and countless people had seen him. This is not an individual who had faked his illness so that Jesus could fraudulently buttress his own messianic credentials. Rather, the man had been indisputably and irremediably crippled and stood in desperate and verifiable need of healing. The longtime and public nature of the man's predicament renders Jesus' healing of this man all the more credible and remarkable. As with the later case of Lazarus, who had been dead for four days, this healing definitely passed the smell test. It was without a doubt a genuine healing.

Now that the stage has been set, the healing ensues. The first thing Jesus does is ask the man, "Do you want to be healed?" (5:6). Well, *of course* the man wanted to be healed! Why did Jesus even bother to ask? Yet Jesus' question did not merely stir the man's will to recover; it also exposed his superstition. "Sir," he replied, "I have no one to put me into the pool when the water is stirred up, and while I am going another steps down before me" (5:7). This verse is probably the reason why some later scribes inserted verse 4 into some later Greek texts, as it alludes to the common superstition of an angel stirring the waters.

To the invalid's mind, his is a futile task. How can he be first in the water when he is unable to walk? Humanly speaking, he'll never be able to access healing. Yet Jesus pointedly cuts straight through any such nonsense, folklore, and superstition, telling the man simply, "Get up, take up your bed, and walk" (5:8). And the man obeys.

In our lives, there may be times when we face seemingly insurmountable obstacles to God meeting our needs or answering our prayers. Yet what we fail to see is that what appears to be impossible to us is possible for God. In Jesus' terms, we need mountain-moving faith (Matt 17:20), or better, we need faith in a God who can move spiritual mountains that we find not only impossible to move ourselves but that we cannot even imagine God can move. But he can!

THE AFTERMATH (5:9B–18)

Interestingly, John has withheld one important piece of information until this very point—namely, that the healing took place on a Sabbath. This is an indication of the deliberate manner in which the Fourth Evangelist has crafted his account. He held off on sharing this piece of information until it became an issue in the story.

At once, the "Sabbath police" (i.e., the Jewish authorities) confronted the man who had just been healed after a thirty-eight-year-long illness. The infraction that drew the leaders' ire was that the invalid, after having been healed by Jesus, picked up and carried his mat or bed, an activity considered work and thus forbidden by Jewish Sabbath regulations (though not Scripture itself).

So what does the healed invalid do when confronted regarding his supposed infraction? He blames Jesus. In effect, his response is: "Don't blame me; blame Jesus!" Well, thanks a lot! Jesus has just graciously and powerfully restored this man's ability to walk, and he repays Jesus by reporting him to the authorities. I wonder if any of you has experienced this kind of ingratitude from someone whom you have helped. I know I have. And it hurt!

When questioned further, the man admits that he doesn't even know who Jesus is or where to find him. Then, a little later, Jesus finds him in the temple area ("find" may or may not imply that Jesus was actually looking for him). Jesus sternly warns the man not to sin any longer so that nothing even worse may happen to him (likely implying that the man's original illness had been due to sin).[11]

---

11. Notice the previously-mentioned contrast with the man born blind in John 9 whose illness was due neither to his own sin nor that of his parents; see the discussion below.

John doesn't record the man's verbal response. He simply tells us that the man at once went to the authorities to tell on Jesus. That's really incredible. Not once, but twice he blames Jesus and tries to get him into trouble. What has Jesus done to deserve this? All he has done is heal the man. That's not only unbelief; it's an inexplicable lack of gratitude.

But have not all of us been guilty of this kind of ingratitude at one time or another? Jesus died on the cross for our sins; yet prior to our conversion, we essentially told him, "Thanks, but no thanks. We're not interested." We all have treated Jesus' sacrifice on our behalf with contempt, or at least indifference.

John goes on to tell us that "this was why the Jews were persecuting Jesus, because he was doing these things on the Sabbath" (5:16). It appears that Jesus deliberately healed on the Sabbath almost as if to provoke the dispute that ensued. Were there not seven days in a week? He could have healed this man and others like him on any day of the week. Why did he have to do it on a Saturday?

Well, he did heal people on other days of the week, as we see in the other Gospels. Not every healing, or even most healings, were performed on a Sabbath. The point here, I believe, is simply that if Jesus encountered a person who required healing, he didn't allow the fact that it was the Sabbath stand in the way of the healing. To do so would have been to capitulate to the unreasonable, petty, and legalistic Jewish stipulations regarding what was or was not permissible on the Sabbath.[12]

Jesus thus used his Sabbath healings to challenge Jewish traditions that were unbiblical and based not on the word of God but on faulty human reasoning and conceptions about God. In this way,

---

12. I realize that in the wake of the "new perspective on Paul" spearheaded by E. P. Sanders it raises eyebrows for anyone to refer to first-century Jews as legalistic, but I believe there continues to be sufficient New Testament evidence to detect works-righteousness and legalism on the part of many Jews we encounter in the New Testament period. See, e.g., John 6:28, where the Jews ask Jesus, "What must we do, to be doing the works of God?" and 6:30: "Then what sign do you do, that we may see and believe you? What work do you perform?" In Paul, see, e.g., Rom 9:32: "Why? Because they did not pursue it by faith, but as if it were based on works."

Jesus asserted his superior knowledge and insight into God's character and requirements. As he said elsewhere, the Sabbath was made for people, not people for the Sabbath (Mark 2:27). And he, being God, had authority over the Sabbath (Matt 12:8; Mark 2:28; Luke 6:5). Thus, the Jewish authorities were correct in discerning that by healing on the Sabbath, Jesus implied he was God.

In the verbal exchange that ensued following Jesus' healing of the lame man in John 5, Jesus declared, "My Father is working until now, and I am working" (John 5:17). Clearly, he put himself on par with God. But what did he mean by his statement, "The Father is working until now?" I believe he here corrected the Jewish assumption that the Sabbath was absolute and that God had forever finished his work. True, the Sabbath commemorated that last day of creation on which God "rested" from his labors, but every child knows that God never sleeps or gets tired and thus truly needs no rest. As Isaiah wrote, "Have you not known? Have you not heard? The LORD is the everlasting God, the Creator of the ends of the earth. He does not faint or grow weary; his understanding is unsearchable" (Isa 40:28). So, as Jesus pointed out, God the Father is continually at work; and in the same way, Jesus, too, was always working—including his work of healing people on a Sabbath if need be.

In the inexorable dynamic of this Johannine narrative, what started out as an innocuous encounter and subsequent healing has slowly but surely morphed into a messianic sign, a pointer to Jesus' authority as the Christ and Son of God. The healing was not primarily about the *invalid* whose ability to walk was restored; it was primarily about *Jesus'* identity as the Christ and Son of God.

Secondarily, the story is also about people's need to respond to Jesus' disclosure of his true identity with personal trust in him. The Jewish leaders who opposed him and took offense at his perceived infraction of their Sabbath rules fell short, as did the man who went off physically healed but spiritually still remained in his sin. His ignorance, unbelief, and outright ingratitude toward Jesus serve as perennial reminders that such abject disregard of Jesus leaves people subject to God's wrath and renders them without excuse. The Fourth Evangelist makes this unfortunate reality explicit when he writes in another aside, "This was why the Jews were seeking all the more to kill him, because not only was he breaking the Sabbath, but he was even calling God his own Father, making himself equal with God" (5:18; cf. v. 16).

FIG. 11: THE REAL REASON FOR JEWISH OPPOSITION TO JESUS (JOHN 5:16, 18)

Passage	Reason for Persecution of Jesus
5:16	"And this was why the Jews were persecuting Jesus, because he was doing these things on the Sabbath."
5:18	"This was why the Jews were seeking all the more to kill him, because not only was he breaking the Sabbath, but he was even *calling God his own Father, making himself equal to God*" (emphasis added).

The issue was ultimately not Sabbath-breaking; the real conflict pertained to Jesus' true identity. As the authorities rightly discerned, by calling God his own Father, Jesus claimed equality with God. However, as the believing reader knows, Jesus was not "making himself" equal to God—he truly *was* equal to God! Yet tragically, the authorities were unwilling to consider this possibility because their hearts were hardened due to their own sin.

Brothers and sisters, we desperately need hearts that are malleable, open, and receptive to who Jesus is and what he wants us to do. A Christian who hates fellow believers or even works actively to bring about their demise is a hypocrite.

You may argue that you don't *hate* other believers. But do you *love* them? Love means giving your life for others as Jesus did and taking positive action on their behalf, not merely ignoring them or even harboring contempt in your heart toward them. We all need to examine our hearts if we desire to learn the lesson John wants to teach us through the story of the invalid and the Jewish authorities who were intransigent toward Jesus because of their sinful, hardened hearts.

CONCLUSION

The healing of the invalid was the first sign of Jesus in the Festival Cycle, which spans John 5–10. The sign sets the stage for the remainder of the Festival Cycle, a literary unit that is marked by escalating antagonism and hostility toward Jesus. The lame man in this account contrasts with the man born blind in John 9, a character who responds very differently to a Sabbath healing. In both cases, the Fourth Evangelist uses these healings as pointers to Jesus' identity as Christ and Son of God, calling his readers to put their faith in Jesus.

Jesus is so worthy of our trust and allegiance. Praise God for the apostle John, who, as Jesus' closest follower during his earthly ministry, gives us a glimpse of Jesus' heart and true identity: Jesus truly is the Messiah and Son of God. These signs are written so that you and I might put our trust in him.

THE FESTIVAL CYCLE

PART 2

The Feeding of the Five Thousand
(John 6)

—

et's continue to explore the dynamic unfolding in the Festival Cycle in John's Gospel. In the previous chapter I pointed out that, generally, John wrote to supplement the other Gospels rather than repeat their material. Where he does use material already included in the earlier Gospels, he usually recasts it to show the deeper theological significance underlying a given teaching or event. I call this John's "theological transposition" of the Synoptic material, similar to what happens in music when a composer transposes a tune from one key to another. Perhaps the most evident example of this are Jesus' signs (*sēmeia*) in John's Gospel, which correspond to his miracles (*dynameis*) in the Synoptics.

In the Synoptics, when the Jewish authorities demand proof for Jesus' messianic authority, Jesus says the only sign he will give is the "sign of Jonah" (Matt 12:38–41; Luke 11:29–32). Jonah was in the belly of the big fish for three days and three nights, which, according to Jesus, prefigured his resurrection. At the same time, the Synoptics record numerous miracles Jesus performed, including demon exorcisms, nature miracles, miraculous healings, and even a couple resurrections (Jairus' daughter: Matt 9:18–26; Mark 5:21–43, Luke 8:40–56; the son of the widow at Nain: Luke 7:11–17). John does not mention the "sign of Jonah" but instead relabels and recasts the Synoptic miracles as signs and records seven of them (the perfect number), culminating in the climactic sign, the raising of Lazarus. This final sign prefigures Jesus' resurrection, which is featured at the end of John's Gospel (John 20–21).

John's transposition of the Synoptic miracles into another key—the seven Johannine signs—is based on the seminal and penetrating theological insight that the primary purpose of Jesus' miracles was not the powerful act itself but the event's function as a signpost to Jesus' messianic identity. In this way, people's responses to Jesus' startling manifestations become a referendum on who Jesus truly is—the Christ and Son of God. We see the same dynamic at work in the second sign of Jesus narrated in the Festival Cycle in John 6, to which we now turn.

THE FEEDING OF THE FIVE THOUSAND (6:1-15)

The feeding of the five thousand is found in all three Synoptic Gospels (Matt 14:13-21; Mark 6:32-44; Luke 9:10b-17). Matthew and Mark also record Jesus' feeding of the four thousand (Matt 15:32-39; Mark 8:1-13). Notably, the details cohere in all four Gospels: the five thousand men plus women and children; the five loaves and two fish; and the twelve basketsful of leftovers. Yet John supplements the Synoptic presentations (which vary to a minor degree) in some significant ways. To begin with, only John features specific disciples by name (Philip and Andrew). Even more importantly, only John includes the ensuing Bread of Life Discourse, which unpacks the christological significance of the feeding and shows how Jesus embodies the sign he has just provided in his very own person—he *is* the living Bread that came down from heaven to give life to the world.

THE SETTING (6:1-4)

As in the case of the healing of the invalid in John 5, John first sets the stage for the sign. Somewhat puzzlingly, John writes, "After this [the Sabbath controversy] Jesus went away to the other side of the Sea of Galilee, which is the Sea of Tiberias" (6:1). This note is puzzling because the previous chapter ended with Jesus being in Jerusalem. The statement "Jesus went away to the *other side* of the Sea of Galilee" seems to presuppose that he had already been at or near the Sea of Galilee.

We have here what you might call a narrative gap. This is merely one of multiple instances in John's Gospel where the evangelist *implies* movement on Jesus' part rather than explicitly narrating it.[1] He expects his readers to have little difficulty in filling in the relevant information that Jesus had traveled from Jerusalem to Galilee in the meantime.

In the earlier Gospels, this body of water is always identified as the Sea of Galilee (even though it is really just a large lake, not an actual sea or ocean). In John's Gospel, however, the same lake is twice referred to as the Sea of Tiberias. This is one of several clues in the Johannine narrative that this Gospel was written later than the other Gospels. We know from extrabiblical sources that the name of the preeminent city on the shores of the Sea of Galilee, Tiberias—named after the Roman Emperor Tiberius (ruled AD 14–37)—was gradually applied to the entire body of water, hence the change in name from Sea of Galilee to Sea of Tiberias.[2] While John here speaks of "the Sea of Galilee, which is the Sea of Tiberias," at the end of the Gospel he simply refers to "the Sea of Tiberias" (21:1).

Jesus' presence in Galilee at Passover is part of the oscillating pattern of Jesus' movements indicated in John's Gospel from Galilee to Jerusalem and back to Galilee (we saw this already in the Cana Cycle [John 2–4], where Jesus went from Galilee to Jerusalem and back to Galilee via Samaria). Here John supplements the Synoptic geographical pattern, according to which Jesus gradually moved from Galilee (where he engaged in multiple concentric circles of ministry) to Jerusalem toward the end of his ministry. In verse 2, John observes that a large crowd was following Jesus because they had seen his previous signs on the sick—presumably including the sign narrated in the previous chapter, the healing of the lame man. In this way, John shows an organic connection between the first two signs of Jesus included in the Festival Cycle.

Yet while the previous sign was a healing miracle, this sign involved Jesus' miraculous ability to multiply food. At the outset, Jesus is shown

---

1. See on this L. Scott Kellum, *The Unity of the Farewell Discourse: The Literary Integrity of John 13:31–16:33*, LNTS (London: T&T Clark, 2004).

2. Cf. Josephus, *Ant.* 18.2.3 §36; Sib. Or. 12:104; *t. Sukkah* 3.9.

to ascend a mountain (6:3, perhaps reminiscent of Moses) together with his disciples. As in the previous case, where John postponed informing readers that the healing took place on the Sabbath, John here postpones mentioning that it was the Passover (6:4). This is now the second Passover narrated in this Gospel; the first was the setting for Jesus' clearing of the temple and encounter with Nicodemus (cf. 2:13, 23). In this way, John continues to use references to various festivals as structural markers in the Festival Cycle in order to show that Jesus fulfilled the entire Jewish festal calendar. Just like Jesus was greater than Abraham, Jacob, and Joseph, and just like he was greater than Moses and the signs and wonders he performed during Israel's exodus, he is greater than all of the Jewish festivals. In fact, he embodies their very essence and constitutes their fulfillment. This is the cumulative point the Fourth Evangelist seeks to drive home in the Festival Cycle in John 5–10.

THE FEEDING OF THE FIVE THOUSAND (6:5–15)

While in the previous chapter Jesus had performed the healing all by himself, in the present instance Jesus' disciples (who were last mentioned in the story of the Samaritan woman in John 4) are integrally involved. This was in keeping with Jesus' pattern of relationship with his disciples depicted in the Synoptics, which in turn was congruent with first-century Jewish rabbi-disciple relationships.[3] Jesus confers with Philip and Andrew (who here, as elsewhere in the Gospel, is referred to as "Simon Peter's brother," cf. 1:40). Andrew mentions a boy with five loaves and two fish but holds little hope that these will go far in feeding such a large number of people. In response, Jesus, rather matter-of-factly, has the people sit down, just as he simply told the man in the previous episode to get up and walk. After giving

---

3. See Andreas J. Köstenberger, "Jesus as Rabbi in the Fourth Gospel," *BBR* 8 (1998): 97–128; Köstenberger, "Jesus as Rabbi" and "The Jewish Disciples in the Gospels," in *A Handbook on the Jewish Roots of the Christian Faith*, ed. Craig A. Evans and David Mishkin (Peabody, MA: Hendrickson, 2019), 178–84, 203–6.

thanks (Grk. *eucharisteō*), Jesus distributes the bread and fish, and everyone eats as much as they want (6:11).

When the disciples gather the leftovers, they fill up as many as twelve baskets (one per disciple). The evangelist notes that "when the people saw the sign that he had done, they said, 'This is indeed the Prophet who is to come into the world!' " (6:14). Thus, the entire pericope (narrative unit) is bracketed by references to Jesus' signs, first to Jesus' healing miracle (6:2) and now to his feeding of the crowd. The reference to "the Prophet" is an allusion to the prophet like Moses mentioned in the book of Deuteronomy (18:15–19).

Perceiving that the people are about to compel him to be their king, Jesus again withdraws to the mountain (6:15; cf. v. 3). Thus, the people in the crowd are the *physical* beneficiaries of Jesus' miracle—they all eat and have their fill—but they fail to grasp who Jesus truly is *spiritually*. Rather than comprehending Jesus' true identity and acknowledging the transcendent nature of his calling, the multitudes conceive of him as a national deliverer. This explains why Jesus withdraws, for he does not want to be co-opted for people's political agenda. As he will later tell Pilate, his kingdom is not of this world (cf. 18:36).

As in Matthew and Mark (though not Luke), John links the account of the feeding of the five thousand with the narrative of Jesus walking on the water (cf. Matt 14:22–32; Mark 6:45–51). While many commentators and study Bibles identify the walking on the water as a Johannine sign, this event is nowhere in John's Gospel identified as such—unlike, for example, the healing of the lame man or the feeding of the multitudes (cf. 6:2, 14). This suggests that while Jesus' walking on the water is a Synoptic-style *miracle*, it is not a Johannine *sign* (notice that Jesus' signs in John are typically *public* while his walking on the water took place *privately*, in front of his disciples alone).[4] Instead, John supplements the account of the feeding of the multitude with the Bread of Life Discourse that ensues.

---

4. See Köstenberger, "Seventh Johannine Sign."

THE BREAD OF LIFE DISCOURSE (6:25–71)

John sets the stage, noting that the event he's recording takes place "on the next day" and "on the other side of the Sea" (i.e., the east side of the lake) in Capernaum (6:22–25). Then, John again records Jesus referring to his signs: "Truly, truly, I say to you, you are seeking me, not because you saw signs, but because you ate your fill of the loaves" (6:26). In other words, people benefited physically from the miracle but failed to perceive the sign and thus missed the true spiritual significance of the event. They failed to draw the necessary connection between Jesus' outward act and the inner spiritual reality of that act— namely, that it identified Jesus as the Christ and Son of God. In the same way, an unbeliever may look at the crucified Jesus with merely human eyes and see a miserable creature die a horrible death while a believer may look at the same crucified Jesus and see him die an atoning death for the sins of humankind.

This is the all-important difference between mere physical seeing and spiritual perception, which the Fourth Evangelist highlights throughout his Gospel. As he said in the prologue, "We [the apostles] perceived [Grk. *theaomai*] his glory" (1:14); and again, following Jesus' inaugural sign, the turning of water into wine at the Cana wedding, "This, the first of his signs, Jesus did at Cana in Galilee, and manifested his glory. And his disciples believed in him" (2:11; cf. 9:3–4). Typically, the Fourth Evangelist points out, people are operating on an earthly plane. Nicodemus only understood earthly things such as natural birth (3:4, 12); the Samaritan woman thought of literal water while Jesus was talking to her about living water, which is emblematic of the Spirit (4:7–15); Jesus offers food his followers know nothing about because his true spiritual "food" is to do the will of the Father who sent him and to accomplish his work (4:34).

Similarly, Jesus here tells the crowd, "Do not work for the food that perishes, but for the food that endures to eternal life, which the Son of Man will give to you" (6:27). Thus, Jesus provides a penetrating commentary on the human condition: We are inexorably caught up in our earthly, physical existence and tied to our need for food, shelter, and clothing (cf. Matt 6:25–34). Yet Jesus—the God-man, the incarnate Son of God—wants to lift people's eyes up from their earthly existence to perceive the heavenly reality to which Jesus came to introduce them. John records people's question to Jesus, "What must we do, to be doing the works of God?" along with Jesus' answer, "This is the work of God, that you believe in him whom he has sent" (6:28–29). In other words, the only "work" God requires is trusting Jesus. And even this trusting response toward Jesus is ultimately God-given (see 6:37 below). It is this total dependence on the one who came to give his life for us that liberates us from our lesser affections, which tie us to our earthly surroundings, posses-sions, and relationships.

Ironically, the crowd applies the same kind of works-oriented, legalistic, self-effort type of thinking not only to themselves but also to Jesus. They ask, "Then what sign do you do, that we may see and believe you? What work do you perform?" (6:30). Again, they put the emphasis on *doing* rather than *being*. Little do they realize that the order is the other way around: Jesus' activity is a mere outflow of his identity; his *doing* flows from his very own *being*. Later Jesus would say, "Believe me that I am in the Father and the Father is in me, or else believe on account of the works themselves" (14:11).

The people proceed to press for proof of Jesus' prophetic creden-tials, probing, "Our fathers ate the manna in the wilderness; as it is written, 'He gave them bread from heaven to eat' " (6:31). By this they allude to the heavenly bread, the manna, that God provided for the Israelites through Moses during their wanderings in the wilderness. If Jesus is the prophet, he must duplicate, if not exceed, the feat Moses wrought during the exodus (cf. 6:15). Can Jesus compete with Moses? The crowd seems skeptical; John's readers know better. Jesus responds first with a correction and clarification: "Truly, truly, I say to you, it was not Moses who gave you the bread from heaven, but my Father gives you the true bread from heaven" (6:32). In other words, it was not Moses who gave the bread to the Israelites in the first place but God; Moses was merely God's instrument. The people were wrong in elevating Moses (or Abraham, or any other previous religious figure) and putting him on a pedestal; all credit belongs to God.

Jesus continues, "The bread of God is he who comes down from heaven and gives life to the world" (6:33). With this, Jesus makes clear that the manna is nothing but a preliminary foretaste of Jesus himself, who is the true antitype and fulfillment of the manna—he is the spiritual "bread from heaven" who will give eternal life to those who believe in him. In this, Jesus provides a remarkable model of explaining the Old Testament with reference to himself (cf. 3:13–14). Similar to the Samaritan woman in John 4, Jesus' audience here entreats him, "Sir, give us this bread always" (6:34; cf. 4:15). Yet Jesus perceives that the people do not understand what they are talking about. They have seen him with their eyes yet have failed to believe in him (6:36). People must look to the Son (6:40), yet they can do so only if the Father gives them to Jesus (6:37). And Jesus will lose none the Father has given him but raise them up on the last day (6:39).

While the crowds were the grateful recipients of the physical food they received from Jesus, they are unwilling to receive the instruction Jesus provides as to the deeper spiritual significance of the sign he has just performed. In this way, the feeding narrative is crucially supplemented by the Bread of Life Discourse. Just like the people who witnessed the temple clearing, these people saw Jesus' sign yet promptly asked for another, making it clear that they failed to perceive the true significance of the original sign (6:31; cf. 2:18). Rather than perform another sign, Jesus proceeds to elaborate on the significance of the sign he has just performed. When he did this previously, he identified his body as the true temple that he would raise in three days. Here, he identifies his body as the flesh and blood that would be given for the life of the world, the nourishment that people must eat and drink in order to receive eternal life.

Rather than clamor for additional signs, demanding ever more evidence for the truthfulness of Jesus' claims, people should come to terms with the evidence he has already provided. An unbelieving attitude that keeps demanding "Give me a sign!" will never be satisfied. In contrast, those who pause to thoughtfully consider the evidence before them will likely find that the evidence they have is more than enough to render a confident verdict. And let's remember—none of us has absolute certainty in a given matter when making a decision. When you buy a car, rent an apartment, or commit to marry the person you love, do you have perfect information? No, you don't. But you don't let that keep you from buying that car, renting that apartment, or marrying that young man or woman. When he calls us to follow him, Jesus presents us with a similar decision. And he doesn't expect us to take a blind leap of faith; he graciously supplies us with abundant evidence that his claims are true. So what are you waiting for? This is an abiding lesson that pertains to us today just as it did to people in Jesus' and John's day.

FIG. 12: THE DYNAMIC OF SIGNS AND DISCOURSES IN JOHN'S GOSPEL

Passage	Original Sign	Request for Sign	Explication of Significance of Sign
2:18–21	Temple clearing	"What sign do you show us?"	Jesus' body is the true temple that will be raised in three days
6:30–33	Feeding of 5,000	"Then what sign will you do?"	Jesus is the true heavenly bread that will give life to the world

In the further interaction that ensues, it becomes increasingly clear that people lack the spiritual perception and openness needed to receive Jesus' difficult teaching. As a result, even many of his disciples no longer follow him. The feeding of the five thousand and the interchange that ensues thus serve as a watershed event in John's Gospel, separating those who follow Jesus merely for superficial, external reasons and temporary personal expediency from those who do so because they have truly perceived that Jesus is the Messiah. The latter comprise Jesus' emergent new messianic community.

When Jesus asks the Twelve, "Do you want to go away as well?" Simon Peter speaks for the entire group when he answers, "Lord, to whom shall we go? You have the words of eternal life, and we have believed, and have come to know, that you are the Holy One of God" (6:67–69). In response, Jesus makes clear that Peter's confession is proof of the Twelve's election. But he goes on to state, rather ominously, that one of the Twelve, Judas, is "a devil"—a traitor who would betray him in order that Scripture may be fulfilled (6:70–71; cf. 17:12).

CONCLUSION

With this, we've come to the end of our study of John's account of the feeding of the five thousand within the overall framework of the Festival Cycle in John 5–10. While John's specific external details of the event cohere with the information given in the other, earlier Gospels, he alone supplements the narrative with an extended discourse. This discourse adds significantly to our understanding of the inner dynamic and deeper purpose of the miracle. In his vintage transposition of the Synoptic presentation, John shows that the feeding is the mere outer shell; the heart of the feeding is the person doing the feeding—Jesus himself. The *physical* bread the multitudes are given to eat is nothing but a pointer to the *spiritual* bread, the Lord Jesus Christ, who came down from heaven to give his life for people as the Lamb of God (cf. 1:29, 36) so that, by believing, they may become God's children and receive eternal life (cf. 1:12).

This is the watershed moment that separates remote followers of Jesus (who enjoy some of the passing temporary benefits of God's provision) from true believers and disciples, who grasp the significance of these benefits and penetrate, by God's grace, to the inner meaning of what these are designed to teach them about Jesus.

Unlike the Synoptics, the Fourth Evangelist includes not a single parable in his Gospel. Yet, in his symbolic discourses, he provides extended comparisons between a natural and a spiritual way of perceiving who Jesus is and what he does. And in so doing, he calls us to attain to the kind of discerning perception of Jesus' messianic nature and mission that enables us to join the ranks of true believers in the Messiah and thus to participate along with them in Jesus' mission in this world. Just as Jesus told his original followers subsequent to the resurrection, he still tells us today, "Peace be with you. As the Father has sent me, even so I am sending you" (20:21).

THE FESTIVAL CYCLE

PART 3

*The Healing of the Man Born Blind
(John 9)*

—

THE FESTIVAL CYCLE

PART 5

The Healing of the Man Born Blind
(John 9)

Afer the watershed moment at the end of John 6—a likely Johannine transposition of Peter's confession at Caesarea Philippi—John 7 finds Jesus briefly at home with his brothers (7:1–9). The scene is reminiscent of Jesus' interaction with his mother at the Cana wedding (cf. 2:1–4). Jesus' brothers do not (yet) believe in him, and they urge him to make a name for himself in Jerusalem (7:3–4). Like his mother, they misjudge the timing of Jesus' public manifestation of his messiahship and reveal that they misunderstand the nature of Jesus' mission (7:6–9).

Thus, at the midway point of the Book of Signs (John 1–12), the picture is bleak: unbelief persists in Jesus' own family and even among his closest followers. The only exception to this unbelief are the Twelve, and even one of the Twelve will turn out to be a traitor. This challenges the perception that failure is an indication we're doing something wrong or, conversely, that success means we're doing something right. Jesus did everything right and backed up his messianic claims with a series of startling signs, yet he was met with massive unbelief.

The Festival Cycle (John 5–10) that began with the healing of the invalid and the feeding of the five thousand in John 5 and 6 (respectively) continues and concludes with four chapters (7–10) that find Jesus at two additional feasts: he is at the feast of Tabernacles in John 7–8 and the Feast of Dedication (or Hanukkah) toward the end of John 10. The four chapters cohere rather tightly.

In some manuscripts, John 7 and 8 are separated by the so-called Pericope of the Adulterous Woman (7:53–8:11), though nearly all scholars believe that this story was added later and was not part of the original Gospel.[1] If this is the case, John 7 and 8 jointly show Jesus initially delaying but then going to the Feast in Jerusalem (7:9–10), appearing in public both at the midway point (7:13–36) and on the final day of the feast (7:37–39). After this, Jesus engages in a second teaching cycle, which culminates in his declaration that he preexisted Abraham (8:12–59). Then, with almost no transition ("As he passed by," 9:1), Jesus encounters a man who had been born blind. The healing, recorded in John 9, is followed by the Good Shepherd Discourse in John 10, again with virtually no transition.

Since Tabernacles is celebrated in September or October and Dedication takes place in December, John 7–10 is concentrated within a fairly short time frame. This indicates that the plot is thickening, as previously the narrative gaps were significantly larger. (Since John 3 had taken place at Passover and John 6 at the next Passover, the healing of the invalid in Jerusalem was the only event John selected for inclusion in almost an entire year of ministry. This shows just how selective John was.) The Festival Cycle concludes with a reference to John the Baptist, who has not been mentioned since John 5.

---

1. See Bruce M. Metzger, *A Textual Commentary on the Greek New Testament*, 2nd ed. (Stuttgart: Deutsche Bibelgesellschaft, 1994), 187–89, who says the evidence against inclusion is "overwhelming" and "conclusive." Craig S. Keener, *John* (Peabody, MA: Hendrickson, 2003), 735–36, concurs that the unit is a later addition based on the textual history and preponderance of non-Johannine vocabulary. See also Gary M. Burge, "A Specific Problem in the New Testament Text and Canon: The Woman Caught in Adultery (John 7:53–8:11)," *JETS* 27 (1984): 141–48; Daniel B. Wallace, "Reconsidering 'The Story of Jesus and the Adulteress Reconsidered,'" *NTS* 39 (1993): 290–96; and William L. Petersen, "οὐδὲ ἐγώ σε (κατα)κρίνω: John 8:11, the *Protevangelium Iacobi*, and the History of the *Pericope Adulterae*," in *Sayings of Jesus: Canonical and Non-canonical: Essays in Honour of Tjitze Baarda*, ed. William L. Petersen, Johan S. Vos, and Henk J. de Jonge, NovTSup 89 (Leiden: Brill, 1997), 191–221.

JESUS AT THE FEAST OF
TABERNACLES (JOHN 7–8)

THE SETTING (7:1–13)

Jesus' public appearance at the Feast of Tabernacles in John 7 and 8 is a perfect example of how John portrays Jesus as fulfilling the very essence of the Jewish festal calendar.[2] The Feast of Tabernacles (also called the Feast of Booths) celebrated God's provision for the Israelites during their wilderness wanderings. The Israelites engaged in water-pouring and torch-lighting rituals to commemorate water coming out of the rock and God guiding his people by a pillar of fire.

For Jesus, the festival is anything but an occasion for Jewish nationalistic pride or even for reliving the past. Rather, he announces that he is the very embodiment of what the Jewish people celebrate. He is one with the God who led Israel at the exodus and will lead his people in a new exodus through his death on the cross. This was not Theology 101; instead, he sought to impart to his listeners a lesson in Advanced Biblical Theology.

HALFWAY THROUGH THE FEAST (7:14–36)

After setting the stage in verses 1–13, John recounts how Jesus made a public appearance at the midway point of the feast. Once again, the evangelist skillfully weaves a reference to a previous event—the healing of the invalid, which commenced the Festival Cycle—into the narrative, giving the account additional coherence and connecting that healing with Jesus' teaching at the feast. "I did one work," Jesus said, "and you all marvel at it. Moses gave you circumcision ... and you circumcise a man on the Sabbath. If on the Sabbath a man receives circumcision, so that the law of Moses may not be broken, are you angry with me because on the Sabbath I made a man's whole body well?" (7:21–23).

---

2. For a lengthy interview I gave on John 7, see "The Light of the World," *White Horse Inn,* June 23, 2019, https://www.whitehorseinn.org/show/the-light-of-the-world.

Thus, Jesus used the classic "from-the-lesser-to-the-greater argument" against the Jewish leaders, who were excessively concerned with the law of Moses but lacked perspective as to its actual purpose. God's purpose for issuing the Sabbath commandment was hardly to keep a longtime invalid from being healed. Jesus gave the example of circumcision, which was performed on the eighth day after a child was born (Lev 12:3). If that day fell on a Sabbath, two commands collided. Should one honor the Sabbath or go ahead with circumcising the infant? Jewish first-century practice held that circumcision was to go ahead; the need to obey the circumcision commandment overrode the command to observe the Sabbath rest.[3]

In this way, a precedent had been set; the Sabbath commandment was not absolute but could be set aside in exceptional cases such as circumcision. Based on this precedent, Jesus argued skillfully against his Jewish opponents that if it was appropriate to circumcise a small part of a person's body, why would it be inappropriate to heal an entire person? Why, for argument's sake, were they too rigid to allow for an exception in this case, which was of obvious benefit to that person and did not truly violate the spirit of the Sabbath command? It is hard to argue with this line of reasoning. In fact, one cannot help but be impressed with Jesus' skillful use of logic and in-depth understanding of Scripture.

At this point, John uses various voices in the crowd at the feast as representatives of variegated Jewish messianic expectations in Jesus' day. "When the Christ appears, no one will know where he comes from," someone opines (7:27); in Jesus' case, they know that he is the carpenter's son from Galilee. A few verses later, someone else queries, "When the Christ appears, will he do more signs than this man has done?" (7:31); this echoes the Jews' previous demands for a sign, particularly at the Bread of Life Discourse (6:31; cf. 2:18). Others query, "Is the Christ to come from Galilee? Has not the Scripture

---

3. See, e.g., Rabbi Yose b. Ḥalafta (ca. AD 140–65): "Great is circumcision which overrides even the rigor of the Sabbath" (*m. Ned.* 3.11; cf. *m. Šabb.* 18.3; 19:1–3).

said that the Christ comes from Bethlehem, the village where David was?" (7:41–43). With fine irony, John here exposes people's ignorance as to Jesus' birthplace. The informed reader knows that what to them appeared to be an obstacle actually confirmed that Jesus was the Messiah, as he had indeed been born in Bethlehem in keeping with Micah's prophecy (cf. Mic 5:2).

In this way, John shows that people were confused—if not conflicted—about who the Messiah would be. Yet Jesus fulfilled all of the scriptural expectations in his messianic identity and mission. The problem was not with anything Jesus was, said, or did; it lay squarely with people's ignorance, confusion, and lack of understanding. Little has changed in the last two millennia in this regard. Today, the problem with people's lack of faith in Jesus is still their lack of understanding of who Jesus truly is and the significance of his actions and teachings, and in particular his death on the cross. However, when Jesus does not fit with our expectations, we should be open to readjust them rather than rejecting Jesus and his claims.

THE FINAL DAY OF THE FEAST (7:37–44)

We've seen how Jesus spoke up at the midway point of the feast. The second occasion John includes is Jesus' appearance on the final day, the "great day" of the feast. Tabernacles festivities lasted for an entire week, and the eighth day ended with a veritable firework of activities. Thus, it is fitting that Jesus makes a final, climactic appearance on the last day of the festival. Issuing an open invitation, he declares, "If anyone thirsts, let him come to me and drink." Not only this, but he adds, "Whoever believes in me, as the Scripture has said, 'Out of his heart will flow rivers of living water' " (7:37–38). John adds that this was a reference to the Spirit who would soon be given. Most likely, the Scripture Jesus is referring to here is a composite from various references in prophets such as Ezekiel. Not only would believers' own thirst be quenched, they would become a Spirit-empowered source of life for others as well.

THE PATERNITY CONTROVERSY (8:12–58)

The Festival Cycle is marked by escalating conflict between Jesus and the Jewish authorities. This was clear from the very beginning, as Jesus and the Jewish leaders clashed when Jesus healed the lame man, sparking the Sabbath controversy (John 5). In what follows, we see yet another controversy erupt between Jesus and the Jewish authorities, which is sometimes called "the paternity dispute." In essence, the debate revolves around the Jewish claim of descent from Abraham.

In John 8, Jesus acknowledges that his opponents are ethnic descendants of Abraham but contends that, spiritually speaking, they are actually the offspring of Satan (8:37–47). This strikes at the heart of Jewish self-understanding. Like so many today, first-century Jews did not generally view themselves as sinners but often put their hope in keeping the law of Moses.[4] Now Jesus argued that their opposition to him—the God-sent Messiah—revealed that their true spiritual paternity could be traced to none other than Satan himself. His reasoning went like this: as Scripture testified, Satan's deception at the fall of humanity brought death. Now the Jewish leaders were plotting to put Jesus to death. In this way, they proved that they were aligned with Satan, who had been "a murderer from the beginning" (8:44). This is strong, explosive stuff! The gloves are off.

Strikingly, John shows that there is no middle ground. People must choose sides; they are either for or against Jesus. You either cast your lot with Jesus, or you are a child of Satan. Neutrality is not an option, as Pilate would soon find out.[5]

---

4. The Synoptics preserve the tradition that first-century Jews spoke of gentiles as "sinners." They did not generally include themselves in this category, as they were God's chosen people. Interestingly, however, John does not feature this contrast, presumably because he believes it to be false. Rather, the Jews are included among the world that has rejected Jesus as Messiah.

5. See Andreas J. Köstenberger, "'What Is Truth?' Pilate's Question to Jesus in Its Johannine and Larger Biblical Context," *JETS* 48 (2005): 33–62; also published as "'What Is Truth?' Pilate's Question to Jesus in Its Johannine and Larger Biblical Context," in *Whatever Happened to Truth?* ed. Andreas J. Köstenberger (Wheaton: Crossway, 2005), 19–51.

THE HEALING OF THE MAN
BORN BLIND (JOHN 9-10)

There is a beautiful symmetry in John's Gospel, which begins with a prologue, ends with an epilogue, and in between presents the story of Jesus in two equal halves, often called "The Book of Signs" (John 1–12) and "The Book of Glory" (John 13–20). The symmetry also extends to the signs in Jesus' two major ministry cycles included in the Book of Signs, namely the Cana Cycle in John 2–4 and the Festival Cycle in John 5–10. In each cycle, we find Jesus performing three signs, and Jesus' movements oscillate between Galilee and Jerusalem. In the Cana Cycle, Jesus turns water into wine at the Cana wedding, clears the Jerusalem temple, and heals the centurion's son back in Cana (2:11, 18; 4:54).

FIG. 13: JESUS' SIGNS IN THE CANA CYCLE
OF JOHN'S GOSPEL

Passage	Sign	Location
2:1–11	Turning water into wine	Cana of Galilee
2:13–22 (cf. 2:23; 3:2)	Clearing the temple	Jerusalem
4:46–54	Healing the official's son	Cana of Galilee

In the Festival Cycle, Jesus heals an invalid in Jerusalem (John 5) and feeds the five thousand in Galilee (John 6). Now, in John 9, we see Jesus perform the sixth sign included in John's Gospel (and the third in the Festival Cycle), when he heals a man in Jerusalem who had been born blind.

FIG. 14: JESUS' SIGNS IN THE FESTIVAL CYCLE
OF JOHN'S GOSPEL

Passage	Sign	Location
5:1–15	Healing the lame man	Jerusalem
6:1–15	Feeding the 5,000	Galilee
9	Healing the blind man	Jerusalem

We can also see John's symmetry in that he includes a set of contrasting characters in both of Jesus' ministry cycles in the Book of Signs: Nicodemus and the Samaritan woman in the Cana Cycle (John 3 and 4) and the invalid and the man born blind in the Festival Cycle (John 5 and 9). This symmetry is less immediately apparent since, unlike Nicodemus and the Samaritan woman, the invalid and the man born blind are not featured in subsequent chapters but rather frame the Festival Cycle; they are the opening and closing signs. But the parallels and contrasts are striking all the same.

FIG. 15: CONTRASTING CHARACTERS IN THE CANA AND FESTIVAL CYCLES OF JOHN'S GOSPEL

Passage	Negative Character	Positive Character
John 3–4	Nicodemus	Samaritan Woman
John 5, 9	Lame Man	Man Born Blind

Notably, both healings take place on the Sabbath. Both are Johannine signs and identified as such, framing, as mentioned, the Festival Cycle. Both involve Jesus' healing of a man in order to manifest his messianic mission.

While the parallels are conspicuous, the contrasts are even more striking. As we saw earlier, the invalid Jesus healed in John 5 is anything but a grateful recipient of Jesus' gracious healing touch. To the contrary, he reports Jesus—not once, but twice—to the Jewish authorities, placing the blame for his alleged Sabbath infraction squarely on Jesus. Also, Jesus sternly warns him not to sin anymore lest something worse happen to him. By contrast, in the case of the man born blind, Jesus immediately makes it clear that neither the man nor his parents had sinned; rather, God had sovereignly ordained his blindness so that God's glory might be revealed in Jesus.

Also, the two men's responses to their respective healings could not be more different. Rather than incriminate Jesus to the authorities, as the lame man had done, the formerly blind man strenuously defends

Jesus against the authorities' accusations. Similar to the Samaritan woman (another fascinating parallel), the formerly blind man first calls Jesus a prophet, later identifies himself as a disciple of Jesus, and finally worships him. This is the only instance of worship directed toward Jesus prior to Thomas' declaration of Jesus as his Lord and God following the resurrection (cf. 20:28).

FIG. 16: COMPARISON BETWEEN THE INVALID AND THE MAN BORN BLIND IN JOHN 5 AND 9

Passage	The Lame Man	Passage	The Man Born Blind
5:11, 15	Reports Jesus to authorities	9:24–33	Defends Jesus against authorities
5:14	Condition a result of sin	9:2–3	Condition not a result of sin
5:10–15	Persists in ingratitude and intransigence	9:17, 27, 38	Calls Jesus a prophet, becomes his disciple, worships him

In this way, the two figures serve as representative characters of contrasting types of faith (or lack thereof). Both are healed by Jesus; nevertheless, a trusting faith response is still required. Yet only the formerly blind man emerges as an example of a person who has been touched by Jesus, responds in faith, and becomes Jesus' disciple and worshiper. In this, too, the formerly blind man echoes Jesus' interaction with the Samaritan woman, whom Jesus instructed regarding true worship in spirit and truth and who becomes an evangelist to her fellow villagers.

The question John is asking his readers is this: How will you respond to Jesus' gracious initiative? Will you respond in faith, like the man born blind (or the Samaritan woman), or will you prove intransigent to Jesus, like the invalid (or Nicodemus)? Will you believe or remain in your sin? That is the all-important question all readers of John's Gospel must ponder.

THE "GOOD SHEPHERD DISCOURSE" (JOHN 10)

The healing of the man born blind segues almost seamlessly into the Good Shepherd Discourse in John 10. The chapter division obscures that there is virtually no transition between the healing narrative and Jesus' discourse. Once again, we see how John accompanies an account of one of Jesus' signs with an extended teaching portion (cf. John 5 and 6).

The Good Shepherd Discourse casts Jesus as the "good shepherd" over against the Jewish leaders, who are irresponsible, self-seeking shepherds as Ezekiel had characterized them in his day (cf. Ezek 34). Thus, Jesus places the Pharisees and himself within a scriptural trajectory of good vs. bad shepherding and aligns himself with God, the shepherd of his people Israel, whom David called "my shepherd" (Ps 23:1; cf. Ps 103:1).

The conversation continues at the Feast of Dedication, which once again highlights Jesus' appearance at Jewish feasts in the Festival Cycle. The Festival Cycle concludes with the *inclusio* involving John the Baptist (10:40–42).

CONCLUSION

With this, we've come to the end of our exploration of the Festival Cycle in John 5–10. As in our study of the Cana Cycle in John 2–4, we've found the Fourth Evangelist to be a careful writer who executes his game plan to perfection. His purpose in his Gospel is to set forth Jesus as the Christ, the Son of God. Toward that end, he has carefully selected a series of startling messianic signs of Jesus.

As we've seen, John has structured Jesus' ministry into an early ministry cycle, the Cana Cycle, and a later ministry cycle, the Festival Cycle. The Festival Cycle is characterized by escalating controversy. In this way, the plot gradually thickens as we become aware that the Jewish authorities take offense at Jesus' claim to be God. In fact, they accuse him of making himself God. We know, however, that Jesus is the preexistent Word-become-flesh.

By being highly selective and by focusing his entire Gospel on the central question of Jesus' identity, John calls each of us to decide: Is Jesus God in the flesh, as his followers came to believe? Or is he a deceiver, blasphemer, and imposter, as the Jewish leaders alleged?

John would have us follow in the footsteps of the Samaritan woman and the man born blind, both of whom encountered Jesus and were profoundly impacted by him. Both made the journey from recognizing Jesus as a prophet to becoming his disciple, evangelist, and worshiper. This is the journey on which you and I should embark. Thank you for joining me on this journey, which will reach new heights in the next chapter.

PART 3

CONCLUSION *to* BOOK OF SIGNS

(JOHN 11–12)

and BOOK OF EXALTATION

(JOHN 13–21)

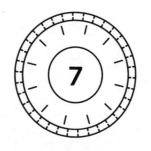

7

CONCLUSION TO THE BOOK OF SIGNS

*The Raising of Lazarus
(John 11)*

—

In the previous chapters, I discussed John's prologue, the Cana Cycle (John 2–4), and the Festival Cycle (John 5–10). The prologue sets the stage for the Gospel in a rather striking way, as it identifies Jesus at the very outset as the eternal Word through whom God created the universe and who in Jesus took on humanity (1:1–5, 14). This Word-made-flesh displayed God's glory in all his words and works and, as God's one and only Son, provided the definitive revelation of God (1:18).

Following the transition from John the Baptist's ministry to Jesus' ministry, which is structured as a "new creation week" marked by repeated references to "the next day" (e.g., 1:29, 35, 43) and finally "the third day" (2:1), we see Jesus embark on an initial ministry cycle, which begins and ends in Cana in the Galilean north. Jesus' two appearances in Cana are poignantly identified as "signs," the first (or inaugural) sign in Cana, and the second sign when Jesus "had come from Judea to Galilee" (2:11; 4:54). In between these two Cana signs, Jesus engages in lengthy interchanges with two contrasting representative figures: Nicodemus, the Jewish Sanhedrin member (3:1–15), and an unnamed Samaritan woman with a checkered past (and present) who, unlike Nicodemus, proves receptive to Jesus' message (4:1–42). Jesus also clears the Jerusalem temple in a prophetic sign symbolizing God's judgment on Israel (2:13–22, esp. v. 18).

The Cana Cycle is followed by the so-called Festival Cycle in John 5–10, which exhibits the escalating nature of Jesus' confrontation with the Jewish leaders. All of this is building up to the crucifixion, which, together with Jesus' resurrection appearances and final interaction with Peter and the "disciple Jesus loved" (the apostle John), forms the climax of the Johannine narrative.

The Festival Cycle shows Jesus at various Jewish festivals, including Tabernacles (John 5; 7–8), Passover (John 6), and the Feast of Dedication (Hanukkah; 10:22). At these religious festivals, Jesus reveals himself as the typological fulfillment of the symbolism inherent in these various feasts. Even though the Jewish authorities tragically reject his claims, Jesus is the true fulfillment of their messianic hopes and expectations.

John clearly shows that the Jewish rejection of Jesus is focused particularly on his claim to deity. In fact, Jesus' claim to deity, and the Jewish authorities' subsequent rejection of this claim, frames the Festival Cycle in John 5 and 10 (respectively). In John 5, this follows Jesus' healing of the lame man on the Sabbath, which resulted in the Pharisees accusing him of egregious lawbreaking and Sabbath violation (see esp. 5:18). In John 10, Jesus' claim follows his healing of the man born blind, another sign performed on the Sabbath (10:30–33).

As we've seen, the lame man in John 5 and the man born blind in John 9 are contrasting characters in that both are healed by Jesus on a Sabbath and yet respond to the healing in diametrically opposite ways: the lame man with brazen ingratitude, the man born blind with discipleship and worship. In between these two framing signs (which resemble the two Cana signs framing the Cana Cycle in John 2 and 4), we see Jesus feeding the multitude in John 6. This messianic sign was reminiscent of God feeding the people of Israel during the exodus when he provided a daily ration of the manna, the "Bread from Heaven." In this case, as elsewhere in John's Gospel, a messianic sign of Jesus is followed by a lengthy explanation of the significance of Jesus' sign—the Bread of Life Discourse.

Jesus' teaching that he is the life-giving bread given by God, which people must eat and whose blood they must drink, proves to be deeply offensive even to many of his own disciples. Some of his followers cease their association with him, and only the Twelve remain (6:60–72). Thus, at the halfway point of the Book of Signs, Jesus' ministry is characterized by a profound note of failure (not that Jesus had failed, but his claims had been met with widespread unbelief).

This motif continues into the second half of the Book of Signs at the beginning of John 7, where even Jesus' half-brothers misunderstand the nature of his messianic calling, and in particular his motives and timing, according to which he was to manifest his messianic identity to the Jewish people and to the world (7:3–6).

The Cana Cycle and the Festival Cycle make up the lion's share of the Book of Signs, which comprises the first half of John's Gospel. Each cycle features three signs of Jesus, one at the beginning and the end of a given cycle, framing the cycle, and another sign in between. The intervening sign serves as a sort of counterpoint in that it is typically in an alternate location from the two framing signs. In the case of the Cana Cycle, the movement is from Galilee to Jerusalem and back to Galilee. In the case of the Festival Cycle, the movement is from Jerusalem to Galilee and back to Jerusalem. In this way, the Fourth Evangelist presents the first six signs of Jesus in the form of an oscillating pattern from Galilee to Jerusalem to Galilee to Jerusalem to Galilee and back to Jerusalem.

FIG. 17: THE BOOK OF SIGNS (OVERVIEW)

Passage	Literary Unit	Major Contents
John 2–4	Cana Cycle	Two Cana signs, temple clearing, Nicodemus and Samaritan woman (three signs)
John 5–10	Festival Cycle	Healings of lame man and of man born blind, feeding of the multitude (three signs)
John 11–12	Lazarus Cycle	Raising of Lazarus (one sign), anointing of Jesus, closing indictment of Jews for rejecting signs

With this, we've arrived at John 11, which narrates the raising of Lazarus from the dead—the seventh and final sign of Jesus in John's Gospel. As we'll see, the raising is followed by a Sanhedrin meeting

(11:45–57), Jesus' anointing by Mary of Bethany—Lazarus' sister—and the plot to kill Lazarus (12:1–11), Jesus' so-called triumphal entry into Jerusalem (12:12–19), and a final episode in which some Greeks come to see Jesus but are deflected by him because his crucifixion (his "lifting up") has not yet occurred (12:20–36a). The Book of Signs closes with the Fourth Evangelist's indictment of the Jewish people, represented by their leaders, who didn't believe in Jesus even though he performed all these messianic signs in their presence (12:36b–50). This will set the stage for the Book of Exaltation, which spans John 13–21.

FIG. 18: THE RAISING OF LAZARUS
AND ITS SIGNIFICANCE

Passage	Literary Unit	Significance
11:1–16	Jesus learns of Lazarus' death	Lazarus' illness "is for the glory of God, so that the Son of God may be glorified through it" (v. 4)
11:17–37	Jesus consoles Lazarus' sisters	They expect Jesus to raise Lazarus at the final resurrection, but he raises him right then! Jesus is "the resurrection and the life" (vv. 24–25)
11:38–44	Jesus raises Lazarus from the dead	Seventh climactic sign of Jesus in John's Gospel prefiguring Jesus' own resurrection

THE RAISING OF LAZARUS (11:1-44)

JESUS LEARNS OF LAZARUS' DEATH (11:1–16)

John's narration of the raising of Lazarus starts out rather innocuously: "Now a certain man was ill, Lazarus of Bethany, the village of Mary and her sister Martha" (11:1). The introduction sounds similar to previous ones in the Gospel, such as that of Nicodemus: "Now there was a man of the Pharisees named Nicodemus" (3:1). Again,

John introduces his readers to a character they are not familiar with from the other, earlier Gospels. This makes his Gospel both enjoyable and interesting to read. In this rather understated way, John begins to tell a truly remarkable story.

While most of John's readers would not have been familiar with Lazarus, many would have recognized Lazarus' sisters, Mary and Martha, who were featured in Luke's Gospel—the well-known story about Martha serving and Mary sitting at Jesus' feet to learn from him (Luke 10:38–42). Even though Martha was likely the older of the two, John here speaks of "Mary and her sister Martha," which may suggest that Mary was the better known or perhaps more highly regarded spiritually for her devotion to Jesus.[1]

FIG. 19: ANOINTINGS OF JESUS IN THE FOUR GOSPELS

Passage	Content	Commentary
Matt 26:6–13	Anointing of Jesus in Bethany by unnamed woman	At Bethany in the "house of Simon the leper"
Mark 14:3–9	Anointing of Jesus in Bethany by unnamed woman	At Bethany in the "house of Simon the leper"
Luke 7:36–50	Anointing of Jesus at Pharisee's house by "sinful woman"	Different anointing by different woman at different juncture in Jesus' ministry
John 12:1–8	Anointing of Jesus by Mary of Bethany	See reference to this anointing in John 11:2 (same as in Matthew and Mark)

Readers who knew about Mary and Martha from Luke's Gospel here learn that the two sisters—who apparently were unmarried—also had a brother, Lazarus (a different Lazarus is featured in Luke's parable of the rich man and Lazarus, the only named character in a parable

---

1. Note, however, that John later speaks of "Martha and her sister" (v. 5) or "Martha and Mary" (v. 19).

in any of the Gospels; cf. Luke 16:19–31). The way John sets the stage for the story indicates that, this time, Lazarus, not his sisters, is the focal character in the narrative.

Then John does something rather striking and unusual. He continues, "It was Mary who anointed the Lord with ointment and wiped his feet with her hair, whose brother Lazarus was ill" (11:2). This note is unusual because the event it refers to—Mary's anointing of Jesus for burial—will not be recorded until the next chapter. How did John expect his readers to know about it? Most likely John assumed his readers were aware of the event from one of the earlier Gospels, which also record that the anointing took place in Bethany along with other consistent details (see Matt 26:6–13; Mark 14:3–9). However, neither Matthew nor Mark identify the woman as Mary—and Luke, who features a story about Mary and Martha, does not record this anointing but rather another one by a "sinful woman," clearly not Mary (cf. Luke 7:36–50). Note also that Luke's story about Mary and Martha simply speaks of Jesus entering "a village" without identifying that village as Bethany (Luke 10:38).

John is helping his readers connect some dots that remain unconnected in the earlier Gospels: he helps us see that the Mary in the story of Mary and Martha and the woman who anointed Jesus for burial in Bethany are one and the same. He also tells us that this pair of sisters had a brother named Lazarus, the focal point in his story. This is an excellent example of John rather skillfully and sophisticatedly complementing the Synoptic Gospels—without contradicting them in any way.[2]

It is also an example of how John seems to assume that his readers are familiar with persons or aspects of Jesus' story from the earlier

---

2. J. J. Blunt (*Undesigned Coincidences in the Writings of the Old and New Testament*, 9th ed. [London: John Murray, 1869]), followed by Leon Morris and others, has called this phenomenon "undesigned coincidences"; however, I would argue that in this case, at least, we have a different phenomenon: John's intentional supplementation of the Synoptics in such a way that he illumines connections between events or characters that had previously remained hidden. Cf. Lydia McGrew, *Hidden in Plain View: Undesigned Coincidences in the Gospels and Acts* (Tampa: DeWard, 2017).

Gospels; how else would we account for John so casually referring to an event he has not yet recounted?[3] John's assumption of his readers' familiarity with the Synoptic account of the anointing is rendered even more plausible by the fact that those accounts of the event end with Jesus' assertion, "Truly, I say to you, wherever the gospel is proclaimed in the whole world, what she has done will also be told in memory of her" (Matt 26:13 = Mark 14:9).[4]

John 11:3 implies that Lazarus' sisters sent messengers to Jesus. Where was he? At the end of the previous chapter, Jesus had withdrawn to the area across the Jordan where John the Baptist had been baptizing (10:40). While he doesn't mention it at 10:40, he previously identified that place as "Bethany across the Jordan" (1:28). Thus, we will see Jesus travel from Bethany across the Jordan to another Bethany, this one located in Judea just outside Jerusalem. So we have here a sort of Bethany Cycle (see the Cana Cycle in John 2–4). The sisters' message to Jesus was: "Lord, he whom you love is ill" (11:3).[5] Later, when Jesus bursts out crying at the sight of Lazarus' tomb, some Jewish bystanders observe, "See how he loved him!" (11:36). It appears that Jesus had a special love for Lazarus and his family, as he shows tender affection for the sisters as well. It is even likely that Jesus regularly stayed with this family when he was in Jerusalem.

Notice that when the sisters sent Jesus this message, Lazarus had not even died; he was most likely seriously ill. In a display of

---

3. Other examples include the reference to Andrew as "Peter's brother" (1:40; cf. 6:8); the parenthetical note that "John [the Baptist] had not yet been put in prison" (3:24); and the casual reference to "the Twelve" midway through the Book of Signs (6:67), even though they had not been previously introduced into the narrative.

4. It is, of course, possible that John expected his readers to have heard this story merely by way of oral proclamation or storytelling, but if he wrote his Gospel a couple decades after the earlier Gospels had been published, it is probably more likely that he presupposed his readers' familiarity with the story from one or both of the written Gospel accounts rather than merely from oral tradition.

5. The fact that Lazarus is here identified as "he whom you love" has caused some to speculate whether Lazarus is in fact the so-called Beloved Disciple, the author of the Gospel, though this is almost certainly wrong. Contra Ben Witherington, "Was Lazarus the Beloved Disciple?" *Ben Witherington* (blog), January 29, 2007, http://benwitherington.blogspot.com/2007/01/was-lazarus-beloved-disciple.html.

supernatural knowledge, when Jesus gets the message, he merely states, "This illness does not lead to death. It is for the glory of God, so that the Son of God may be glorified through it" (11:4). Notice how here Jesus puts himself—the self-identified Son of God—on par with God and asserts that both God and the Son of God will be given glory through the healing that would ensue. In his disposition toward adversity (albeit not in his divine nature), Jesus is a great example for all of us; we, too, should view adversity as an occasion for God to glorify himself. When we receive what appears to be bad news, is our natural reaction, "This happened so that God may receive greater glory"? Unfortunately, no; but by the grace of God and through the work of the Holy Spirit, it can be our *supernatural* reaction!

In another puzzling statement, John says, "Now Jesus loved Martha and her sister and Lazarus. *So, when he heard that Lazarus was ill, he stayed two days longer in the place where he was*" (11:5–6, emphasis added). Any of us who hears about a loved one's serious illness would rush to their side at once, but not Jesus. How are we to reconcile the two statements that seem utterly contradictory—that Jesus *loved* Lazarus and his sisters and that *he stayed where he was two extra days*? This defies human logic and makes Jesus seem rather uncaring. Yet, as we saw at the Cana wedding or Jesus' delayed departure to the Feast of Tabernacles, Jesus marches to a different drum and cannot be pressured to intervene until he determines that the time is right.

This story is highly relevant to those who are awaiting an answer to prayer. When we're experiencing a major illness or other emergency, we may feel perplexed that God is not hearing our desperate cry for help. Why is God delaying when our need is so acute? We don't understand. And yet, will we trust that God makes all things beautiful in his time? God is never late—even when it appears that he is.

Likewise, in the present story, Jesus is not late; he only *appears* to be. In fact, delaying his departure and subsequent arrival at the scene only means that he gets there four rather than two days after Lazarus has died. To be sure, his delay causes the sisters additional anguish, but at the same time, it enables Jesus to raise Lazarus from the dead a full *four days* after Lazarus had died. This was widely believed to be impossible, as, according to common first-century Jewish belief, a person's spirit left their body three days after death.

As is usual in the Gospels, Jesus' disciples are rather slow on the uptake (as I'm sure I would have been as well). When Jesus, after two days' delay, tells them, "Let's go to Judea again," they reply, "Rabbi, the Jews were just now seeking to stone you, and are you going there again?" (11:8; cf. 10:33). As good followers of their rabbi, the disciples are rightly concerned for their teacher's safety, so they discourage him from going to Jerusalem—he might get himself killed! Ironically, Jesus *will* get killed in (or just outside) Jerusalem. But Jesus insists he must go there anyway (11:9–10).[6]

And then, in a further case of misunderstanding (or lack of understanding), Jesus tells the disciples, "Our friend Lazarus has fallen asleep, but I go to awaken him," at which they reply that if he has merely fallen asleep, he will recover (11:11–12). So Jesus tells them plainly, "Lazarus has died" (11:14). Jesus intends to use this incident to strengthen his disciples' faith in him. Rather than fear for his life (though he will eventually die), they should learn how to believe in the Messiah who can heal the lame, feed the hungry, open the eyes of the blind, and even raise the dead (cf. Isa 35:5–6; 42:7).

Then doubting Thomas, rather sarcastically and no doubt with gallows' humor, remarks, perhaps under his breath, "Let's also go, that we may die with him" (11:16). In this case, "him" probably refers to Jesus, though less likely it may refer to Lazarus. "Things seem to be going down the drain anyway" seems to be Thomas' sentiment, so what if Jesus' ill-advised journey to Judea hastens his demise?[7]

---

6. Later, we see Paul similarly disregard the warning of a prophet named Agabus who warns him of his upcoming arrest and go on to Jerusalem nonetheless (Acts 21:10–12; cf. 11:27–28).

7. Some scholars disagree and portray Thomas' statement as an expression of loyalty and courage, though this seems less likely, especially in light of Thomas' later display of a skeptical attitude following the resurrection (20:25–28).

JESUS CONSOLES LAZARUS' SISTERS (11:17–37)

In verse 17, Jesus arrives in Bethany, marking stage two of the Johannine narrative (and possibly hinting at a Bethany Cycle; cf. 1:28; 10:40; and see above). There is implied movement between verses 16 and 17 in that in verse 16, Thomas is saying, "Let's also go, that we may die with him," and in verse 17 we read, "Now when Jesus came." In the interim, Jesus and his followers apparently traveled the dusty road from Bethany near the Jordan to Bethany near Jerusalem.

Even though John doesn't make this connection explicit, we might argue that this is another *inclusio* that ties the Book of Signs together in a large ministry cycle "from Bethany to Bethany." Thus, we could view the entire Book of Signs as the Bethany Cycle, spanning from John's initial baptizing ministry to Jesus' raising of Lazarus. Jesus, and the entire Johannine narrative, have come a long way from those early days of Jesus' mission. In the interim, he has performed six messianic signs and is about to perform a seventh, climactic sign. John's Gospel continues to display his brilliant literary composition skills.

In the original Greek, the emphasis in the statement "Now when Jesus came, he found that Lazarus had already been in the tomb four days" falls squarely on "four days" (11:17). It seems that Jesus arrives at the scene way too late. If there were ever hope that Jesus might keep Lazarus from dying, there is no hope now. Or is there?

John then offers a helpful detail for his readers outside of Palestine who may have been unfamiliar with the lay of the land. He explains that "Bethany was near Jerusalem, about two miles off" (11:18). Many of Mary and Martha's friends had made the journey from Jerusalem to console them (11:19).

Upon Jesus' arrival, we see Lazarus' two sisters take diametrically opposite courses of action, highlighting their difference in personalities. Martha at once goes to meet Jesus—in fact, she goes ahead to meet Jesus before he ever gets to Bethany (11:30). Mary, on the other hand, "remained seated in the house"—she was, as Jews would call it today, "sitting *sheva*" for her brother, maintaining a seated posture of mourning that customarily lasted for an entire week.

Martha's words to Jesus are intimate, trusting, and perhaps a touch wistful: "Lord, if you have been here, my brother would not have died. But even now I know that whatever you ask from God, God will give you" (11:21–22). Jesus responds that her brother will live again (11:23), to which Martha replies that she knows Lazarus will come back to life at the final resurrection (11:24). Jesus then tells her, "I am the resurrection and the life. Whoever believes in me, though he die, yet shall he live, and everyone who lives and believes in me shall never die. Do you believe this?" (11:25–26). Martha replies, "Yes, Lord, I believe that you are the Christ, the Son of God, who is coming into the world" (11:27).

We can register several observations here.

First, Martha's statement here perfectly anticipates John's purpose statement toward the end of the Gospel (cf. 20:30–31). Thus, Martha serves as an example of the kind of faith in Jesus that John writes his entire Gospel to engender in others.

Second, we see that here, as elsewhere (e.g., John 6), a messianic sign performed by Jesus is coupled with an "I am" statement—in the present case, "I am the resurrection and the life." In this way, John stresses that Jesus, in his very own person, embodies the essence of what he demonstrates in performing a given sign. Just like he doesn't merely feed the multitudes by giving them bread but is *himself* the life-giving Bread, so Jesus will not merely raise Lazarus from the dead but is in *himself* the resurrection and the life. As John asserted in his prologue, "In him [Jesus] was life" (1:4). In John 5 Jesus declared, "For as the Father raises the dead and gives them life, so also the Son gives life to whom he will. ... Truly, truly, I say to you, an hour is coming, and is now here, when the dead will hear the voice of the Son of God, and those who hear will live. For as the Father has life in himself, so he has granted the Son also to have life in himself" (5:21, 25–26). With these preceding statements, Lazarus is poised to serve as the climactic example of one who hears Jesus' word and receives life. In John 5 Jesus further said, "Truly, truly, I say to you, whoever hears my word and believes him who sent me has eternal life. He does not come into judgment, but has passed from death to life" (5:24). The story of Lazarus thus serves as a living illustration of Jesus' earlier assertion that those who hear his word and believe in him have eternal life. Who needs parables anyway?[8]

Third, Jesus' claim to have life in himself is an astonishing, momentous assertion that amounts to a claim to deity; for none other than God has life in himself. He alone is the uncreated, eternal, ever-living God. As a student in Sunday School might say, God is the "eternal liver"! And not only does Jesus live eternally, but he has been granted authority, and thus has the ability, to give eternal life to everyone who hears his word and believes in him. On a literal level, this was true for Lazarus, who had died a literal death and had already been in the tomb for four days when Jesus restored him to life.

Fourth, the present account marks John's Gospel as the "Gospel of life," over against the earlier Gospels that focused on Jesus' proclamation of God's kingdom. In this we see John's universalizing tendency. While "kingdom" had nationalistic and ethnic overtones, harking back to the kingdoms of David and Solomon, "life" is a universal characteristic that pertains to every person. To cite Shakespeare's famous quote, "To be, or not to be, that is the question."[9] John would more likely declare, "To believe, or not to believe, *that* is the question." The raising of Lazarus serves as the epitome of John's purpose statement: "Now Jesus did many other signs in the presence of his disciples, which are not written in this book; but these are written so that you may believe that Jesus is the Christ, the Son of God, and that by believing you may have life in his name" (20:30–31).

Fifth, Martha here serves as the representative of conventional Jewish expectations in her day as she states that her brother will be raised "in the resurrection on the last day" (11:24). But Jesus asserts that he will raise Lazarus right then and there. In this way,

---

8. I've noted previously that parables are absent from John's Gospel. Instead, John uses real-life stories to demonstrate the truthfulness of Jesus' statements.

9. William Shakespeare, *Hamlet*, Act 3, Scene 1.

Jesus epitomizes John's realized eschatology. In Jesus, the kingdom is already here and has already been inaugurated. The raising of Lazarus serves as a living demonstration that the eternal Life-Giver, Jesus, is already present with humanity. What is more, life—eternal, spiritual life—is a gift to be enjoyed already in the here and now, not merely in some distant future day.

Do you believe this? Do you believe that you can enjoy eternal life—full, abundant life—already in the here and now? And are you living and experiencing this full, abundant life that Jesus came to bring? Are you living in the knowledge that, since you believe in Jesus, you will not come into judgment but have already passed from death into life? All of your guilt has been taken away by Jesus, the Lamb of God who has taken away the sin of the world. You are now, and forever, free to live for and with him. That's terrific news! So let's make sure we proclaim it and pass it on to others.

Far too many preachers and sermons still neglect this realized aspect of Jesus' coming that John is so adamant to highlight. So let's make sure we preach and teach that in Jesus, the future has already invaded the present. Eternal life is not merely a future hope and expectation—it is a present reality that believers in Jesus are privileged to experience now and for all eternity.

Following her momentous interchange with Jesus, Martha tells her sister Mary that Jesus is calling for her (11:28). At this, Mary quickly goes to meet Jesus (11:29). Some of Mary's Jewish friends who had come to mourn with her follow along, thinking she is going to the tomb; providentially, this throng of fellow mourners provides a substantial "cloud of witnesses" to the messianic sign Jesus is about to perform. When Mary speaks to Jesus, her words are identical to her sister's: "Lord, if you had been here, my brother would not have died" (11:32; cf. 11:21). How devoted and trusting these two sisters were toward Jesus!

Underlying the sisters' words is deep sorrow over their beloved brother's death. It is evident how loved Lazarus was, by both Jesus and his two sisters. Blessed is the man who is so much loved by God and others! John then notes that Jesus is both "deeply moved in his spirit" (Grk. *embrimaomai*) and "greatly troubled" (Grk. *tarassō*) when he sees Mary and those consoling her weep and mourn (the repeated Greek word is *klaiō*, "weep").[10] He asks them to take him to the tomb. We can see in this account the skillful way in which John continues to build drama and suspense by slowly narrating Jesus' progression from outside the village to the tomb.

JESUS RAISES LAZARUS FROM THE DEAD (11:38–44)

Jesus, "deeply moved again," at last arrives at the tomb (11:38). The Greek verb *embrimaomai*, which is translated as "deeply moved," may connote Jesus bristling at death as a horse might do. Jesus is bracing himself to confront death itself! John Calvin says he is like "a wrestler preparing for the contest"; "no wonder that he groans again," Calvin says, "for the violent tyranny of death which he had to overcome stands before his eyes."[11]

The tomb is described as a cave with a stone rolled against it, a typical tomb (11:38). Yet here and in the narrative that follows, the vocabulary used anticipates the narration of Jesus' own burial later on in John's Gospel. John wants us to see a connection between the two accounts and to read the raising of Lazarus as a sneak preview of Jesus' own death, burial, and resurrection.

Jesus calls for the stone to be taken away, at which, Martha—whom John calls "the sister of the dead man"—gently warns Jesus that "there will be an odor" as her brother has already been dead four days (11:39).[12] John thus reminds his readers of the magnitude of the challenge Jesus is facing. He is about to raise a man who has been dead for four days—enough time that his body has already begun to decay

---

10. Note that the words "deeply" and "greatly" are added in the ESV. There is no additional Greek word (adverb) to convey the intensity of Jesus' emotions. Rather, it is implied in the Greek verbs *embrimaomai* and *tarassō*.

11. John Calvin, *The Gospel according to St. John 11–21*, trans. T. H. L. Parker, ed. D. W. Torrance and T. F. Torrance (Edinburgh: Oliver & Boyd, 1961), 13.

12. "Dead man" or "deceased" is in the Greek pluperfect participle, underscoring the permanence of Lazarus' condition.

and emit the odor of decay and corruption. Lazarus wasn't merely dead—he was totally and seemingly irrevocably dead. Yet Jesus is undaunted, a picture of utter resolve and determination.

You can cut the tension with a knife now; the drama is almost too much to bear. "Did I not tell you that if you believed you would see the glory of God?" Jesus tells Martha, challenging her to keep faith now (11:40). As they roll away the tombstone, Jesus prays, as is his custom at such occasions. He prays in part to convey his dependence on God the Father in his earthly mission and in part for the benefit of those who were about to witness arguably the greatest messianic sign Jesus ever performed (11:41–42).[13]

We've now reached the climactic moment in both the narrative and the historical sequence of events leading up to the present moment. When he is finished uttering his short prayer, Jesus simply cries out "with a loud voice [literally, 'a great voice'], 'Lazarus, come out!' " (11:43). Like the original witnesses of this historical event, we await with bated breath what will happen next. Will this turn out to be a colossal failure? Or will the dead man really come back to life? Consider the striking simplicity of Jesus' command. Three simple words, that's all—"Lazarus, come out"—directed toward a dead person. Would the dead person obey Jesus' command?

At once, John relieves the tension by reporting, "The man who had died came out, his hands and feet bound with linen strips, and his face wrapped with a cloth." Jesus then directed the bystanders, "Unbind him, and let him go" (11:44).

That's it! It's all so matter-of-factly and so tersely narrated. Lazarus is the main character of the narrative, yet he has been silent, dead and lying in his tomb for the duration of the entire narrative—until now, the very end, the climax of the story. He appears, his hands and feet still bound with linen strips and his face still wrapped in a cloth.

---

13. Note, of course, that the resurrection of Jesus was even greater, but I would argue that it was not itself a sign but rather the reality to which this and other signs (such as the temple clearing) pointed. See my article "The Seventh Johannine Sign: A Study in John's Christology," *BBR* 5 (1995): 87–103.

John 11:44 is one of my favorite statements in all of John's Gospel, if not the entire Bible: "The dead man came out"(NRSV). The dead man came out! Obviously, he was no longer dead. Can you imagine a more subtle way of narrating a resurrection? "The dead man came out."[14] There were no trumpets, no fanfare—just a simple command to remove the strips of linen and the face cloth so Lazarus could walk again. It is almost comical to imagine how Lazarus must have struggled to walk with the strips of linen tying his hands and feet still in place.

Just picture the incredible scene the witnesses of this amazing messianic sign of Jesus were privileged to behold: Lazarus, the man who had been dead for four days—and whom people had mourned for—walked out of the tomb, from the darkness of the cave into broad daylight, from death into life, from literal bondage and decay into freedom. In this way, Lazarus serves as a representative of all who believe and as a result pass from death into life, as Jesus envisioned in his earlier comments in John 5 (cf. 5:24).

CONCLUSION

We could say so much more about this seventh and final messianic sign of Jesus in John's Gospel—the only sign that is a resurrection and as such prefigures, like no other sign, the resurrection of Jesus himself at the end of John's narrative. But with this, we have completed our study of the seven signs of Jesus in the first half of John's Gospel—the so-called Book of Signs. The number seven, here as elsewhere in John's writings, serves to convey the notion of perfection and completeness.

The raising of Lazarus is an amazing miracle in itself. But more importantly, it serves as a signpost to who Jesus is in his very essence: "I am the resurrection and the life" (11:25). And like the previous six

---

14. Cf. the similarly subtle reference to "the water now become wine" in 2:9 at Jesus' first sign at the Cana wedding.

signs, this seventh, climactic sign was recorded so that we, the readers of John's Gospel, may believe that Jesus is the Messiah and Son of God.

God doesn't want us just to marvel at the greatness of the sign itself—the fact that Jesus raised a man who had been dead for four days, a feat that stands unique in human history. No, *the greatness of the sign is dwarfed by the greatness of the one who wrought it*—Jesus, the Messiah, the Son of God, the one who alone can raise the dead and who can give eternal life to everyone who believes.

Let me ask you the same question Jesus asked Martha: Do you believe this (11:26)? This is more than a mere spiritual truth to be affirmed in abstract fashion as part of a creed or statement of faith. It requires personal trust and life commitment to the Giver of Life, Jesus, who can guard what we've entrusted to him until that final day when God will execute judgment and raise the dead for all eternity so that those who have placed their faith in Christ will live with him for all eternity.

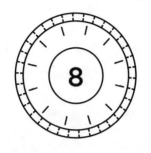

JESUS' PREPARATION OF HIS NEW MESSIANIC COMMUNITY

The Farewell Discourse
(John 13–17)

I n our study of John's Gospel thus far, we've seen how John presents Jesus performing a series of seven messianic signs, culminating in the greatest of them all: the raising of Lazarus, who had been dead four days. What more could Jesus have done to prove that he really was the long-awaited Messiah? This is precisely the point that John drives home as he concludes the first half of his Gospel, the Book of Signs: "Though he [Jesus] had done so many signs before them," John writes, "they [the Jewish people] still did not believe in him" (12:37). John adds that the Jews' unbelief in Jesus fulfilled Isaiah's prophecies that the Jews didn't believe despite a series of mighty acts of God, which ultimately was the result of divine hardening: "Therefore they could not believe. For again Isaiah said, 'He has blinded their eyes and hardened their heart, lest they see with their eyes, and understand with their heart, and turn, and I would heal them' " (12:39–40).

Sound familiar? Just as God performed mighty miracles during the exodus, delivering his people from bondage in Egypt and providing daily sustenance in the wilderness, so now Jesus has performed mighty works during his ministry, announcing people's deliverance from spiritual bondage to sin and identifying himself as the spiritual food and drink that would sustain God's people if they only placed their faith in him. Yet, the nation of Israel, represented by the Jewish religious leaders, has rejected the abundant evidence Jesus has provided for them. They have rebuffed Jesus' claim to deity, denied seven selected messianic signs of Jesus, and proven that they are tragically hardened in their hearts so that they cannot perceive Jesus' true identity and believe and be saved. What more could God the Father, and Jesus his Son, do to reveal themselves? Nothing.

John thus frames the entire Book of Signs (John 1–12) as an exercise in *theodicy*—the demonstration that the responsibility for people's unbelief lay not with God but with the people and their sin-hardened hearts. And yet, paradoxically, John argues that even though people were fully responsible for rejecting the Messiah despite the great and irrefutable body of evidence he had presented, people's hardness of heart and rejection of the Messiah were nonetheless God's own doing.

Notice that it doesn't say, "Therefore they *would* not believe," but rather, "Therefore they *could* not believe" (12:37, emphasis added). How can God be sovereign and yet still hold people responsible for their choices? Good question! On our limited, finite plane of logic, this seems to be a paradox, if not an oxymoron or outright contradiction. Only from God's point of view can such two apparently irreconcilable propositions be reconciled as both being true—a view some call "compatibilism."[1]

In any case, halfway through the Gospel, John has already closed the book on the Jewish people, who are represented by their leaders. Similar to the closing of John 6, the halfway point of the Book of Signs, John 12 closes the first half of John's Gospel on a profound note of failure. Jesus' messianic mission to the Jews has failed.

Or has it? In a sense, it has, in that the nation as a whole, led by the Sanhedrin, will shortly pronounce the guilty verdict over Jesus, convicting him of blasphemy for his fraudulent claim to deity (or so they thought). In another sense, however, as we saw at the end of John 6, there is a silver lining: the Twelve, Jesus' new messianic community, which represents a believing remnant in the long-anticipated Messiah who has now come in Jesus. We see this clearly in a fascinating parallel between John's prologue and the preamble to Act II in John's Gospel drama, a literary unit I call the Book of Exaltation. In the prologue, John had written,

---

1. See, e.g., D. A. Carson, *Divine Sovereignty and Human Responsibility: Biblical Perspectives in Tension* (Atlanta: John Knox, 1981; reprint, Eugene, OR: Wipf & Stock, 2002).

He was in the world, and the world was made through him, yet the world did not know him. He came to his own, and his own people did not receive him. But to all who did receive him, who believed in his name, he gave the right to become children of God. (1:10–12)

Now, in the preamble to the second half of the Gospel, John writes,

Now before the Feast of the Passover, when Jesus knew that his hour had come to depart out of this world to the Father, having loved his own who were in the world, he loved them to the end. (13:1)

In both passages, John uses the poignant phrase "his own." In the prologue this phrase refers to the Jewish people—"his own people" who "did not receive him," but in the preamble to the Book of Exaltation this phrase refers to the believing remnant—the Twelve—who were "his own who were in the world." Jesus loved this believing remnant to the end—he loved them completely and to the utmost extent by giving his life for them as the Good Shepherd (cf. John 10). And it is this believing remnant, the new messianic community, whom Jesus prepares in John 13–17, the so-called Farewell Discourse, prior to his departure on the eve of the crucifixion.

THE FAREWELL DISCOURSE: INTRODUCTORY MATTERS

The Farewell Discourse (or Upper Room Discourse) is unique to John's Gospel. It is yet another example of how John masterfully supplements the earlier Gospels. Matthew, Mark, and Luke relate the Last Supper and Jesus' institution of the new covenant in his body and blood with the Twelve (Matt 26:17–30; Mark 14:12–26; Luke 22:7–39). But only John treats us to an extended, behind-the-scenes glimpse of how Jesus prepared his followers for the trying time that lay just around the corner.

THE FAREWELL DISCOURSE AND THE
FAREWELL SPEECH GENRE

The Farewell Discourse seems to be loosely patterned after Moses' farewell speech to the people of Israel on the verge of entering the promised land in the book of Deuteronomy. John thus adds to the series of parallels he has presented between Jesus' ministry—including his messianic signs—and the people of Israel during the exodus (see, e.g., John 6).[2] Just as the people of Israel in Deuteronomy were on the verge of entering the promised land, where they would experience the fruit of God's mighty deliverance, so the Twelve are on the verge of experiencing God's mighty deliverance through Jesus' cross-death and resurrection. And just like the Israelites needed instruction on proper conduct once delivered, so did the Twelve.

In the Farewell Discourse, as in the book of Deuteronomy, we see a pronounced emphasis on the disciples' need to "keep" and "obey" God's commands and to love God and others.[3] In this way, both Deuteronomy and the Farewell Discourse cut straight to the heart of the pervasive biblical message: God's love for his people and his desire for them to reciprocate his love and for them to love both God and others.[4] This is epitomized particularly in the "new commandment" Jesus gives his disciples, which is that they are to love one another as he loved them (13:34–35; cf. 1 John 2:7–11).

Apart from Moses' farewell discourse, we find multiple farewell speeches in the Old Testament. For instance, we see them in the patriarchal narratives in the book of Genesis (see esp. Gen 49) as well as in Joshua 23–24, 1 Samuel 12, 1 Kings 2:1–12, and 1 Chronicles 28–29. Once we arrive at the Second Temple literature (i.e., Jewish writings dating to the second century BC until the end of the first century

---

2. See also my remarks on 12:37–40 above.

3. See esp. John 14:15, 21, 23, 24; 15:9–13, 17, where "keep" and "love" terminology converges and is featured abundantly. Cf., e.g., Deut 6:2, 4, 17; 7:7, 9, 12; 8:2, 6, 11; 28:9, 45; 29:9; 30:8, 10, 16; 30:6.

4. I hope to develop this further in a forthcoming biblical theology.

AD), we find that farewell discourses had become a full-fledged literary genre. This is particularly evident in the work *Testaments of the Twelve Patriarchs*, which is built off the patriarchal farewell speeches in the book of Genesis.

Typically, farewell addresses include most (if not all) of the following components:

+ Predictions of death and departure

+ Predictions of future challenges sons or followers of a dying man would encounter after his death

+ Arrangements regarding the continuation of the family line or succession

+ Exhortations to moral conduct

+ A final commission

+ A reaffirmation and renewal of God's covenant promises

+ A closing doxology[5]

In the Farewell Discourse in John's Gospel, Jesus announces his departure (though, significantly, he predicts his return after "a little while").[6] He envisages future challenges his followers will face after his departure, particularly persecution for confessing Jesus as Messiah (15:18–16:4). He makes arrangements for succession, which in his case involves sending "another Helping Presence," the Holy Spirit, who would not only be *with* them as Jesus was during his earthly mission, but who would be *in* them, that is, spiritually indwell them, thus marking an actual advance in the closeness of his disciples

---

5. See Francis J. Moloney, *The Gospel of John*, SP 4 (Collegeville, MN: Liturgical Press, 1998), 377–78.

6. Cf. 13:33; 14:19; 16:16–19.

with the Triune God.[7] Jesus also exhorted his followers to moral conduct, urging them to keep his commands, particularly the "new commandment" to love one another the way he had loved his followers (13:34–35). Jesus also uttered a final prayer and anticipated a later commission of his followers when he prayed to the Father, "As you sent me into the world, so I have sent them into the world" (17:18; cf. 20:21). In this way, we see John appropriating and adapting the "farewell discourse" genre, with particular salvation-historical retrieval of the book of Deuteronomy.

STRUCTURE

As we look at the Farewell Discourse in John's Gospel in its entirety, we can discern its structure as follows:

13:1–30	Footwashing Narrative: Cleansing of the New Messianic Community
13:31–16:33	Farewell Discourse: Preparation of the New Messianic Community
13:31–14:31	First Cycle of Instruction: The "Other Helping Presence"
15:1–16:33	Second Cycle of Instruction: Vine and Branches, the World's Hatred
17	Final Prayer

The Farewell Discourse opens in John 13 with the account of the footwashing, which serves as an anticipatory glimpse of the love Jesus displayed when dying on the cross for the sins of the world. It is an

---

7. 14:15–18. On the Trinitarian dimension, see Andreas J. Köstenberger and Scott R. Swain, *Father, Son and Spirit: The Trinity and John's Gospel*, NSBT 24 (Downers Grove, IL: InterVarsity, 2007).

example of the Johannine love ethic.[8] Then, the narrative turns into discourse—mostly monologue that is occasionally interrupted by questions from Jesus' disciples (John 14–16). The final chapter (17) is devoted to Jesus' high-priestly prayer, which is a unique feature among farewell discourses.

Within the Farewell Discourse proper (13:31–16:33) we can discern two cycles of instruction with some overlap in topic (e.g., that Jesus provides instructions regarding the coming of the Holy Spirit in both cycles). The end of the first cycle is marked by Jesus telling his disciples, "Rise, let us go from here" (14:31). This may imply movement away from the upper room and toward the garden of Gethsemane; alternatively, Jesus could be urging his disciples to depart with him but is delayed from doing so until the end of John 17. It wouldn't be the first time that someone says "Let's go" when invited to someone's house and then stays for another half hour before actually leaving!

The second instruction cycle (John 15–16) illustrates Jesus' continuing spiritual relationship with his disciples in the Spirit by using the metaphor of a vine and its branches. Jesus represents the vine—an image prominently used for Israel in the Old Testament (e.g., the "Song of the Vineyard" in Isa 5)—and the disciples the branches, who must continually be connected to the vine in order to bear spiritual fruit and avoid drying up spiritually.

---

8. To which I address an entire chapter in my Johannine theology. See Andreas J. Köstenberger, *A Theology of John's Gospel and Letters,* BTNT (Grand Rapids: Zondervan, 2009), ch. 13.

FOOTWASHING NARRATIVE: CLEANSING OF THE NEW MESSIANIC COMMUNITY (13:1–30)

FROM THE EARTHLY TO THE EXALTED JESUS

Chapter 13 marks a radical change in perspective in John's Gospel. From the opening of the Gospel to the end of John 12, John presents Jesus' mission from an *earthly* vantage point: Jesus seeks to prove himself to the Jews as the God-sent, long-anticipated Messiah. But starting with John 13, John adopts the vantage point of the *exalted* Jesus who anticipates his departure to God the Father and the resumption of his preexistent glory following his death, burial, and resurrection.

FIG. 20: TWO BOOKS OF JESUS IN JOHN'S GOSPEL

Passage	Major Literary Unit	Primary Perspective
John 1–12	Book of Signs	The mission of the earthly Jesus to the Jews: seven selected messianic signs
John 13–21	Book of Exaltation	The mission of the exalted Jesus to the world: new messianic community in the power of the Spirit

John even presents the crucifixion from a vantage point that differs from that of the earlier Gospels. Those Gospels emphasize the shame and humiliation Jesus endured for our sake. Yet John, strikingly, presents the cross as a place of triumph and exaltation, as a place where God the Father was glorified and Jesus was, to use language from Isaiah, "lifted up" (see esp. Isa 52:13: "Behold, my servant shall act wisely; he shall be high and lifted up, and shall be exalted"). This is underscored particularly by the three "lifted up" sayings in John's Gospel (3:14; 8:28; 12:32), as John reveals with ever-greater specificity that Jesus would be "lifted up," both literally at the cross and spiritually by divine exaltation.

FIG. 21: "LIFTED UP" SAYINGS IN JOHN'S GOSPEL

Passage	"Lifted Up" Sayings	Commentary
3:14	"And as Moses lifted up the serpent in the wilderness, so the Son of Man must be lifted up"	Exodus typology with Numbers 21: Jesus' "lifting up" analogous to Moses' lifting up bronze serpent in the wilderness
8:28	"When you have lifted up the Son of Man, then you will know that I am he"	Jesus to people who do not understand his otherworldly origin (descent-ascent motif)
12:32	"And I, when I am lifted up from the earth, will draw all people to myself"	Aside in 12:33 explains: "He said this to show by what kind of death he was going to die." The crowd think Messiah will remain forever.

Each time Jesus utters a "lifted up" saying, his listeners are incredulous and fail to grasp his otherworldly origin. As such, these three sayings are part of the descent-ascent motif in John's Gospel, which stresses that Jesus entered the world from his preexistent glory and that he would return to the glory he had with the Father before the world began (17:24). The preamble to the Book of Exaltation (the second half of the Gospel of John) makes clear that John adopts this otherworldly vantage point in telling the remainder of Jesus' story:

Now before the Feast of the Passover, *when Jesus knew that his hour had come to depart out of this world to the Father,* having loved his own who were in the world, he loved them to the end. During supper, when the devil had already put it into the heart of Judas Iscariot, Simon's son, to betray him, Jesus, *knowing that the Father had given all things into his hands, and that he had come from God and was going back to God,* rose from supper. He laid aside his outer garments, and taking a towel, tied it round his waist. Then he poured water into a basin and began to wash the disciples' feet. (13:1–5, emphasis added)

John presents the cross as only a station on Jesus' way back to the Father and his heavenly glory. Jesus had "come from God and was going back to God," that was it! Oh, and on the way back to God, Jesus was going to make a quick stop at the cross so he could die for the sins of the world. And at the cross, Jesus would be "lifted up," that is, exalted as the obedient Son of the Father who completed his mission.[9] So we'll see Jesus report back to God in his final prayer, "I brought glory to you here on earth by completing the work you gave me to do" (NLT 17:4, an *inclusio* with 4:34). And on the cross, he'll cry out, "It is finished" (Grk. *tetelestai*; 19:30). In this way, John sets the cross in proper perspective and recasts it as a place of glory and exaltation rather than shame and humiliation.

THE FOOTWASHING AS AN INTRODUCTION TO THE PASSION NARRATIVE

The footwashing itself is not only a self-contained literary unit, but it is also part of the introduction to the Johannine passion narrative (John 18–20). In other words, we see at the footwashing the perfect love that caused Jesus to give his life for sinful humanity (13:1).

On the eve of the crucifixion, Jesus engages in a didactic action, which was not uncommon for first-century Jewish rabbis.[10] In washing his disciples' feet, Jesus startles his followers and arouses their curiosity. How could he, their teacher, stoop to such a lowly task—one

---

9. See Andreas J. Köstenberger, *The Missions of Jesus and the Disciples according to the Fourth Gospel* (Grand Rapids: Eerdmans, 1998).

10. See Andreas J. Köstenberger, "Jesus as a Rabbi in the Fourth Gospel," *BBR* 8 (1998): 97–128; Köstenberger, "Jesus as Rabbi," and "The Jewish Disciples in the Gospels," in *A Handbook on the Jewish Roots of the Christian Faith*, ed. Craig A. Evans and David Mishkin (Peabody, MA: Hendrickson, 2019), 178–84, 203–6.

that was customarily reserved for menial household slaves? In this way, Jesus deliberately provokes his followers to reflect on the true meaning of leadership: they must see it as servanthood out of humility and heartfelt, God-inspired love.

Judging from the other Gospels, this is a lesson his disciples desperately needed to hear and heed. It is one that we still need to hear and heed today.[11] Leadership is not about self-promotion. It's not about building our own platform, peddling our own wares, or recruiting others to serve our own agenda. It's about seizing upon existing, real needs and rising to meet them even if it is inconvenient or causes us to get our hands dirty.[12] As Jesus said, "I have given you an example [Grk. *hypodeigma*], that you also should do just as I have done to you. Truly, truly, I say to you, a servant is not greater than his master, nor is a messenger greater than the one who sent him. If you know these things, blessed are you if you do them" (13:16–17).

In the context of John's Gospel, and more narrowly the Farewell Discourse, the footwashing shows the cleansing of the new messianic community. This cleansing was both physical—they needed to have their dirty feet washed in a culture where you wore sandals and walked long distances on dusty roads—and spiritual. In conjunction with the Passover meal that followed, the footwashing also served to expose Judas the betrayer, whose feet Jesus graciously washed but who at the end of the meal slipped into the night (13:30), signifying the dark errand he was about to run. With this, the new messianic community—the believing remnant, Jesus' "own"—was cleansed and ready to be instructed about the trying but ultimately joyous days ahead.

---

11. Cf., e.g., Matt 18:1–4; Mark 9:33–36; Luke 9:46–47; 22:24–30.
12. Cf., e.g., the parable of the good Samaritan (Luke 10:25–37).

FAREWELL DISCOURSE:
PREPARATION OF THE NEW
MESSIANIC COMMUNITY (13:31–16:33)

FIRST CYCLE OF INSTRUCTION:
THE "OTHER HELPING PRESENCE" (13:31–14:31)

The underlying logic of the Farewell Discourse is that, counterintuitively, not only would the disciples not be seriously disadvantaged by Jesus' imminent departure, but it would actually be better for them if Jesus went away. Initially, this was a non-starter with the disciples. How could it possibly be better for them to be without Jesus, whose constant presence they had grown accustomed to over the past three and a half years? Yet Jesus strenuously argues that his physical presence will be replaced with the Spirit's continual spiritual presence, which knows no limits in time and space.

Thus he tells his followers, "I will ask the Father, and he will give you another Helper, to be with you forever, even the Spirit of truth, whom the world cannot receive, because it neither sees him nor knows him. You know him, for he dwells with you and will be in you. I will not leave you as orphans; I will come to you" (14:16–18). He continues, "The Helper, the Holy Spirit, whom the Father will send in my name, he will teach you all things and bring to your remembrance all that I have said to you" (14:26).

In this way, Jesus prepares his disciples for the time after his departure. Once he has been exalted, the Spirit will continue Jesus' work in and through his followers. Jesus thus makes provision for his succession and ensures that the mission of the Triune God will continue uninterrupted. The opening words of the book of Acts come to mind: "In the first book, O Theophilus, I have dealt with all that Jesus began to do and teach" (Acts 1:1). Luke implies that, now, he will tell the story of what Jesus *continued* to do and teach. It is possible that John read Luke-Acts and mirrors the two-part structure in the Book of

Signs and the Book of Exaltation.[13]

SECOND CYCLE OF INSTRUCTION:
VINE AND BRANCHES, THE WORLD'S HATRED (15:1–16:33)

After the so-called Johannine *aporia* (or alleged literary seam) at the end of John 14 ("Rise, let us go from here"), the Farewell Discourse enters a second cycle of instruction. Similar to the Good Shepherd Discourse in John 10, Jesus here uses a corporate metaphor to teach a vital spiritual truth about his followers' connection with him. In John 10 he used the imagery of a shepherd and his flock, focusing on the intimacy between the shepherd and his sheep and on his commitment to protect his followers spiritually from all harm. Now, in the context of his teaching on the coming of the Holy Spirit, Jesus explains to his disciples what for them was going to be an entirely new reality: life in the Spirit.[14]

He illustrates the vital, organic union that the Spirit will help them sustain with Jesus by using the familiar image of the vine and the branches. This image clearly hearkens back to Old Testament depictions of Israel as God's vineyard, most famously Isaiah's "Song of the Vineyard" (Isa 5). Significantly, the present scenario depicts Jesus himself as God's vine and his followers as branches of that vine. They must remain vitally connected to Jesus and his teachings, of which the Spirit will remind them (14:26). They also must remain in his love (15:9). They cannot bear fruit by themselves. In fact, apart from Jesus, they can do nothing (15:5). The term "fruit," I believe,

---

13. See Andreas J. Köstenberger, "John's Transposition Theology: Retelling the Story of Jesus in a Different Key," in *Earliest Christian History: History, Literature, and Theology; Essays from the Tyndale Fellowship in Honor of Martin Hengel*, ed. Michael F. Bird and Jason Maston, WUNT 2/320 (Tübingen: Mohr/Siebeck, 2012), 191–226.

14. A couple decades later, the apostle Paul would take instructions on "life in the Spirit" to new heights in Romans 8. See Gregg R. Allison and Andreas J. Köstenberger, *The Holy Spirit*, Theology for the People of God (Nashville: B&H Academic, 2020), esp. 139–45.

encompasses both ministry fruit (including converts) and character fruit (growth in Christlikeness).

Love for Jesus and for one another will be particularly essential as the world hates Jesus' followers. Again, the maxim pertains: "'A servant is not greater than his master.' If they persecuted me, they will also persecute you" (15:20; cf. Matt 10:24). Therefore, Jesus' followers must bear witness in the power of the Holy Spirit (John 15:26–27). Jesus tells the disciples that they will be expelled from the synagogue, and in fact, "the hour is coming when whoever kills you will think he is offering service to God" (16:2; cf. 9:22, 34–35).[15] I greatly appreciate Jesus' candor in this regard. Too often today we are under the impression that people will receive the gospel message with open arms. Some may, but many others will vehemently oppose it. In fact, not only will they oppose it, but they will persecute the messengers because the world of which they are a part—incited by Satan, the "ruler of this world" (12:31; 14:30; 16:11)—hates Jesus and thus will hate his messengers as well.

FINAL PRAYER (17)

It is highly significant that the Farewell Discourse closes with an extended prayer. This is uncommon for farewell discourses but shows Jesus' dependence on God the Father in accomplishing his mission. It also demonstrates the essential unity between Father and Son in carrying out that mission. As Jesus had asserted at the height of his conflict with the Jewish leaders, "The Father and I are one" (10:30). Yet, in the divine economy, it is the Son, not the Father, who is the

---

15. Advocates of the Johannine community hypothesis have taken references to synagogue expulsion in John's Gospel as indications that here the Johannine community anachronistically imposed its own story (AD 90s) onto the story of Jesus (AD 30s). See esp. J. Louis Martyn, *History and Theology in the Fourth Gospel*, 3rd ed. (Louisville: Westminster John Knox, 2003) and many of his followers. However, note that here the reference is in the future in the form of a prediction of Jesus. In 9:22, 34–35, the reference is to an impulsive act by the Jewish authorities who expel the formerly blind man from the local synagogue in an effort to intimidate him. This should not be taken as reflecting the kind of official policy that stipulated the expulsion of Jewish Christians—those who believed that Jesus was the Messiah predicted in the Old Testament—from local synagogues in the AD 90s (the so-called *birkat-ha-minim* or "curses on the heretics").

point person in the divine redemptive mission, the *missio Dei*, and it is the Son, not the Father, who dies on the cross for our sins. It is also the Father who sent the Son, not the Son who sent the Father. In the mysterious economy of the inner workings of the Trinity, we see here that the divine persons are united and equal in personhood yet distinct in the roles they fulfill within God's plan of salvation.

FIG. 22: JESUS' FINAL PRAYER (JOHN 17)

Passage	Prayer Focus	Major Contents
17:1–5	Jesus himself	Jesus (the Sent One) reports to the Sender (God the Father) that he has successfully completed his earthly mission
17:6–19	Jesus' disciples	Jesus prays for his followers who are in but not of the world; he prays for their unity and spiritual protection
17:20–26	Future converts	Jesus also prays for those who would become believers through the witness of his new messianic community

Jesus' final prayer proceeds in three phases. He first prays for himself (17:1–5); then for the disciples (17:6–19); and finally for those who would become believers through the disciples' witness (17:20–25). This is yet another amazing and unique contribution John makes to the Gospel canon in the New Testament. Jesus' prayer for himself acknowledges that this is the hour of his glorification: "I glorified you on earth, having accomplished the work that you gave me to do. And now, Father, glorify me in your own presence with the glory that I had with you before the world existed" (17:4–5).

The prayer offers a fascinating glimpse into Jesus' (and John's) theology of glory. Jesus brought God glory through everything he said and did during his earthly ministry (not just the signs). But in addition, he is about to bring glory to God by dying on the cross. It is not as though the cross constitutes a shameful interruption of God's glory. To the contrary, the cross is the climax, the supreme moment of Jesus' glorification, as it is at the cross that we see the culmination of the obedient Son's mission. Just as we take pride in the completion of a project, so Jesus is elated at the imminent prospect of completing his work on the cross.

In those final moments before the crucifixion, therefore, Jesus focuses not on the pain he will soon suffer but on the eternal glory that awaits him and those he will save. He views the cross as the indispensable pathway and entryway to glorious, eternal life with the Father. In this way, John gives us a new set of spiritual glasses and teaches us to look at the cross in an entirely new way. Properly understood, the cross marks "*Good* Friday" because of the benefits that it accrues for sinful humanity and also because of the glory it brings to God the Father and Jesus the Son.

I'll conclude my all-too-brief discussion of the Johannine Farewell Discourse with a short discussion of what I consider to be the underlying burden of Jesus' final prayer—the mutual love and spiritual unity of the new messianic community, which is to be grounded in the mutual love and spiritual unity among the members of the Trinity themselves. Jesus' burden is this: "I do not ask for these only, but also for those who will believe in me through their word, that they may all be one, just as you, Father, are in me, and I in you, that they also may be in us, so that the world may believe that you have sent me" (17:20–22). If we, as God's people, are not unified and do not love one another, how can we expect our mission to be successful?

CONCLUSION

We do not have the space to adequately explore the many spiritual dynamics that are in play throughout the Farewell Discourse. We marvel that John, by including this unique set of materials, has raised our spiritual understanding of life in the Spirit and of the meaning of the cross to a whole new level. We have seen how the footwashing provides a sneak preview of the love that caused Jesus to die on the cross for the sins of the world. We also saw how it serves the purpose of cleansing the new messianic community.

By gathering the believing remnant—the Twelve minus Judas—and by instructing his followers about the future, Jesus makes provision for succession. His redemptive mission, accomplished at the cross, will continue unabated in the mission of his followers as undergirded by the mission of the Holy Spirit.

In the final chapter, I will explore John's passion narrative, including Jesus' commission of his disciples and his final words to Peter and the "disciple Jesus loved."

9

THE JOHANNINE PASSION NARRATIVE AND EPILOGUE

(John 18–21)

—

It has been a joy and a pleasure to walk through John's Gospel with you. Most recently, we engaged in a close reading of the narrative of the raising of Lazarus, the seventh messianic sign of Jesus. We also studied the Farewell Discourse in John 13–17, the first half of what I call the Book of Exaltation. We've seen that in this fascinating and largely unique section, John significantly complements what we know from the earlier Gospels about Jesus' final hours prior to the crucifixion.

We've also come to appreciate how John radically shifts perspective from Jesus' earthly mission to the Jews in the Book of Signs (John 1–12) to an exaltation vantage point in the Book of Exaltation (John 13–21). All that remains for us to do now is to pick up the narrative in 18:1 and to read together through the rest of John's Gospel, the so-called Johannine passion narrative, as well as the account of Jesus' resurrection appearances, John's purpose statement, and the epilogue in John 21.

The narrative breaks down into the following major sections:

FIG. 23: MAJOR SECTIONS IN THE JOHANNINE PASSION NARRATIVE

18:1–11	Betrayal and Arrest
18:12–27	Informal Hearing before Annas, Peter's Denials
18:28–19:16a	Roman Trial before Pilate
19:16b–42	Crucifixion, Death, and Burial
20	The Empty Tomb, Resurrection, and Commission
21	Epilogue

Within these broader sections, John alternates in the second unit (18:12–17) between the informal hearing before Annas, the Jewish high-priestly patriarch (18:12–14, 19–24), and Peter's denials (18:15–18, 25–27). Jesus' Roman trial before Pilate unfolds in two stages: (1) an initial interrogation culminating in a not-guilty verdict (18:28–38a) and (2) a final summons culminating in the death sentence against Pilate's better judgment due to Jewish pressure (18:38b–19:16).

Remarkably, John all but skips Jesus' Jewish trial, which is the primary focus in the Synoptic accounts. The only thing John says about Jesus' formal Jewish trial is that "Annas then sent him [Jesus] bound to Caiaphas the high priest" (18:24). This gives us the unmistakable impression that John writes to supplement the Synoptics by, on the one hand, providing material that the Synoptics do not (or only briefly) cover while, on the other hand, assuming that his readers have knowledge of the material presented in the Synoptics.

Proportionately, John gives more attention to Jesus' Roman trial, which may reflect the fact that only Pilate could legally pronounce the guilty verdict punishable by crucifixion and that Pilate, along with the Jewish Sanhedrin, represented the world's rejection of Jesus, whom Pilate derisively calls "the king of the Jews." These distinctive Johannine emphases unfold within the common historical framework of the final events in Jesus' earthly mission attested to in the previous Gospels.

BETRAYAL AND ARREST (18:1–11)

The story of Jesus' so-called arrest is already well documented in the Synoptics. Following the Farewell Discourse, Jesus and his disciples cross the Kidron Valley just outside Jerusalem and enter what John refers to as merely a "garden" (18:1). Those familiar with the earlier Gospels know that this is the garden of Gethsemane, a large, walled-in olive grove. John notes that Jesus had often met with his disciples in this garden, which explains why Judas knows where to find Jesus on the night of the crucifixion (18:2).

The appearance of Judas accompanied by "a band of soldiers and some officers from the chief priests and the Pharisees with lanterns and torches and weapons" (18:3) is almost comical—a total overkill. It implies that Jesus was a dangerous criminal whose arrest would require an overwhelming force. To the contrary, not only does Jesus offer no resistance, but he initiates the arrest and is shown to be sovereignly in charge throughout the proceedings. In this way, John underscores that God is sovereign throughout the passion narrative and that Jesus is innocent of all the charges brought against him.

The way John sets the stage for the arrest—"Then Jesus, knowing all that would happen to him" (18:3)—follows seamlessly the preamble to the Book of Exaltation, where John similarly asserted that Jesus knew where he had come from and where he was going (13:1–3). None of the proceedings against him take Jesus by surprise. In this, John concurs with the Synoptics, who record Jesus' repeated predictions of his passion and demise.

When Jesus identifies himself as "I am" to the arresting motley crowd, they respond as if they are experiencing a theophany (a manifestation of God); they draw back and fall to the ground (18:6). Considering that John would have been an eyewitness to the arrest, this is an astonishing account that attests to the supernatural power Jesus must have exuded at this pivotal event. Once again, similar to Jesus bracing himself to confront death at Lazarus' tomb, we see deity refracted through frail humanity on full display.

In what follows, John also highlights the fulfillment of what Jesus spoke to his disciples earlier in the Johannine narrative (18:9; cf. 6:39). Also, in the scene where Peter draws his sword and cuts off the high priest's servant's ear, John notes it is his right ear and identifies the servant as Malchus (18:10). Again, John here supplements information provided in the earlier Gospels, which had not given the name of the servant. Typically, one would have expected earlier accounts to provide more specificity such as names or other details, so the fact that John here is more specific and detailed than the earlier Gospels is remarkable. One possible reason might be that Malchus or members of his family were still alive when the earlier Gospels were written (notice the mention of a relative in 18:26). If so, it is possible, if not likely, that the Synoptics sought to protect his anonymity (and thus safety) by withholding his name (on the assumption that they knew it). By the time John wrote, however, Malchus would have likely passed away, removing the need to protect his identity. This idea of "protective anonymity" was propagated by the German scholar Gerhard Thiessen and popularized by the British scholar Richard Bauckham in his work *Jesus and the Eyewitnesses*.[1]

INFORMAL HEARING BEFORE ANNAS AND PETER'S DENIALS (18:12–27)

In this next section (18:12–17), the Fourth Evangelist moves back and forth between the informal hearing before Annas, the Jewish high-priestly patriarch (18:12–14, 19–24), and Peter's denials (18:15–18, 25–27). In many ways, this is not unlike the way movies are made today, shifting back and forth from one scene to another, which once again attests to John's narrative skill, literary art, and deliberate storytelling and structuring in his material. The following oscillating pattern is the result:

FIG. 24: OSCILLATING STRUCTURE IN JOHN 18:12–27

18:12–14   Informal hearing before Annas
    18:15–18 Peter's first denial
18:19–24   Informal hearing before Annas (cont.)
    18:25–27 Peter's second and third denials

John's account of Jesus' hearing before Annas includes yet another detail left out in the Synoptics. Only John mentions Annas as having

---

1. Richard Bauckham, *Jesus and the Eyewitnesses: The Gospels as Eyewitness Testimony*, 2nd ed. (Grand Rapids: Eerdmans, 2016).

any part in Jesus' Jewish trial, though Luke (always the careful historian) notes that John the Baptist's and Jesus' ministry took place "during the high priesthood of Annas and Caiaphas" (Luke 3:2). How could there have been two high priests? John clarifies that Annas was "the father-in-law of Caiaphas, who was high priest that year" (John 18:13). This makes clear that Caiaphas was the actual high priest while Annas was his still-influential father-in-law. In addition, John reminds us of Caiaphas' earlier comment that "it would be expedient that one man should die for the people" (John 18:14; cf. 11:49).

The Synoptics already attested to Peter's threefold denial of Jesus, though there are some minor differences with regard to the cock crowing and so on that need not detain us here. In John, however, this threefold denial is later matched by Peter's threefold confession of love for Jesus and Peter's reinstatement to ministry (21:15–19). In addition, notice that in both cases, the scene takes place near a charcoal fire (Grk. *anthrakia*; 18:18; 21:9). This provides a subtle yet unmistakable detail that links Peter's threefold denial and threefold reinstatement and frames the entire passion narrative (John 18–21).

Annas questions Jesus about his teaching and his disciples, implying that Jesus had operated covertly. Jesus rightly retorts that he had always taught openly in public places, "in synagogues and in the temple, where all Jews come together" (18:20); he could hardly be accused of leading a covert insurrection. Again, Jesus stays calm and in control and clearly has the upper hand in the interchange.

ROMAN TRIAL BEFORE
PILATE (18:28–19:16)

We now move on to Jesus' Roman trial, which, while covered in the earlier Gospels, receives more expansive treatment in John's Gospel, especially when compared to the Fourth Evangelist's coverage of the Jewish trial, which he virtually passes over. John presents Jesus' trial before the Roman governor Pilate in two phases: (1) an initial interrogation culminating in a not-guilty verdict (18:28–38a); and (2) a final summons culminating in the death sentence, which Pilate decrees against his better judgment due to Jewish pressure (18:38b–19:16). The discrepancy between the initial verdict of not guilty and the final verdict of guilty highlights the inconsistency and many fatal flaws of the judicial proceedings against Jesus, notable in a Roman context that prided itself for its sophisticated state of jurisprudence and the rule of law:

FIG. 25: TWO PHASES OF JESUS' TRIAL BEFORE PILATE

18:28–38a	Initial Interrogation: "Not guilty"
18:38b–19:16	Final Interrogation and Verdict: "Guilty"

Let me make a few observations on the exceedingly important passage culminating in Pilate's question, "What is truth?" (18:38).[2] First off, John mentions that when the Jews handed Jesus over to the governor, they didn't enter his house so as not to defile themselves. This rings true historically and culturally but most likely is an instance of Johannine irony as well. The Jewish authorities handed over the Messiah to be crucified but were scrupulous to keep Jewish purity regulations so they could celebrate their religious rituals. Incredible! Also, while they considered Pilate an unclean gentile, they needed his cooperation to get Jesus crucified.

When it comes to their charges against Jesus, there seems to have been a certain "progression" (not to mention disingenuousness). They first vaguely identify him as a man "doing evil" (18:30). When Pilate doesn't take the bait and tells them to judge Jesus by their own law, they up the ante until they eventually acknowledge the true reason why they find Jesus so offensive: "We have a law," they tell Pilate, "and

---

2. For a detailed exegesis and exposition of this exceedingly important passage, see my essay: Andreas J. Köstenberger, "'What Is Truth?' Pilate's Question to Jesus in Its Johannine and Larger Biblical Context," *JETS* 48 (2005): 33–62. See also Köstenberger, "Introduction," "'What Is Truth?' Pilate's Question to Jesus in Its Johannine and Larger Biblical Context," and "Epilogue," in *Whatever Happened to Truth?* ed. Andreas J. Köstenberger (Wheaton: Crossway, 2005), 9–17, 19–51, 131–36.

according to that law he ought to die because he has made himself the Son of God" (19:7). Again, we see here the charge we encountered earlier: that Jesus "made himself" the Son of God (cf. 5:18; 10:33). In other words, he arrogated the exalted status of deity while being a mere man. He was a self-made man, self-appointed, motivated by self-interest. Yet, to the contrary, Jesus has continually affirmed in John's Gospel that it was God who sent him on his mission and that he came to give his life sacrificially for the benefit of others rather than to pursue his own agenda.[3]

Another important element in John's account is Jesus' insistence before Pilate that his "kingdom is not of this world" (18:36). Even Pilate kept mocking Jesus as "king of the Jews," no doubt wondering how this rather pitiful-looking creature before him could possibly be the political threat to Roman rule the Jewish authorities made him out to be. One can almost hear the sarcastic tone in Pilate's voice when he summons Jesus again: "Are *you* the King of the Jews?" (18:33, emphasis added). In this way, the Roman governor did not merely mock Jesus but sneered condescendingly at the entire Jewish nation.

The ensuing interchange then revolves around the nature of Jesus' kingship. This is telling, especially as, in distinction from the Synoptics, Jesus is not presented as proclaiming the coming of the "kingdom of God" but rather as the giver of "eternal life." The phrase "kingdom of God" occurs in John's Gospel only in Jesus' conversation with Nicodemus (3:3, 5).

We find three major characters in Jesus' Roman trial before Pilate: the Jewish authorities, Pilate, and Jesus.[4] John portrays the *Jewish authorities* as hypocritical, insincere, and manipulative. Through political maneuvering and disingenuous scheming, they eventually

---

3. On God the Father having sent Jesus, see, e.g., 5:37; 6:44; 7:16; 8:29, 42; 12:49; 20:21. On Jesus giving his life for others, see esp. the Bread of Life Discourse (John 6), the Good Shepherd Discourse (John 10), and the footwashing (John 13), as well as John the Baptist's depiction of Jesus as the Lamb of God who takes away the sin of the world (1:29, 36). On Jesus' work, see my *Mission of Jesus and the Disciples*, chap. 3, esp. 52–80.

4. For a detailed analysis of these three major characters, see Köstenberger, "What Is Truth?"

convince Pilate to change his mind and pronounce a guilty verdict. Thus, they succeed in having the hated Romans crucify the Messiah on a trumped-up charge and in swaying the crowds. *Pilate*, for his part, represents the futile effort to remain neutral with regard to Jesus. By avoiding making a decision, he makes one nonetheless: to reject Jesus and to condemn him to die. *Jesus*, finally, is in firm control in the face of severe adversity; he is calm, constant, and unfazed by both the Jewish and the Roman authorities. He remains silent when charged with blasphemy (19:9), reminiscent of Isaiah's Servant of the Lord (cf. Isa 53:7),[5] and he tells Pilate that he would have no authority had it not been given to him from above (John 19:11).

In the crucible of intense testing and suffering, Jesus emerges unscathed spiritually and ultimately victorious, while the powers of this world—both Jewish and Roman, representing the world at large—prove to be corrupt and guided by nothing but personal and political self-interest. In a chilling reprise, soon after Jesus' crucifixion and resurrection, Peter and John would bear witness to the risen Jesus before Annas and the Jewish Sanhedrin. When released, they lifted their voices in prayer, citing a Davidic messianic psalm:

> "Sovereign Lord, who made the heaven and the earth and the sea and everything in them, who through the mouth of our father David, your servant, said by the Holy Spirit,
>
>> 'Why did the Gentiles rage,
>>   and the peoples plot in vain?
>> The kings of the earth set themselves,
>>   and the rulers were gathered together,
>>   against the Lord and against his Anointed'—
>
> for truly in this city there were gathered together against your holy servant Jesus, whom you anointed, both Herod and Pontius Pilate, along with the Gentiles and the peoples of Israel,

---

5. See also Peter's depiction of Isaiah's "Servant of the Lord" in his suffering (1 Pet 2:21–25; cf. Isa 52:13–53:12).

to do whatever your hand and your plan had predestined to take place." (Acts 4:24–28; cf. Ps 2:1–2)

Thus Peter, John, and the early Christians came to realize that the Jewish-gentile conspiracy against the Messiah fulfilled Old Testament prophecy. They also came to believe that it was ultimately not Pilate and the Sanhedrin but God himself who had predestined what would take place in the events leading up to Jesus' crucifixion. On the basis of this twofold conviction, they concluded their prayer and received a remarkable answer to their prayer:

> "And now, Lord, look upon their threats and grant to your servants to continue to speak your word with all boldness, while you stretch out your hand to heal, and signs and wonders are performed through the name of your holy servant Jesus." And when they had prayed, the place in which they were gathered together was shaken, and they were all filled with the Holy Spirit and continued to speak the word of God with boldness. (Acts 4:29–31)

When was the last time your church prayed and at the end of that prayer the place where you were gathered was shaken and all were filled with the Holy Spirit?

Returning to John's passion narrative, it is hard to imagine a starker contrast between Jesus, "the light of the world" (John 8:12), and the dark forces that pin him to the cross. In the end, Pilate, in his official function as Roman governor of Judea, sits down on the judgment seat (Grk. *bēma*) and pronounces Jesus guilty despite the lack of legitimate charges against him (19:13). We recognize that a serious travesty of justice has just transpired. The Jewish authorities tragically betray their own messianic hope, crying, "We have no king but Caesar!" (19:15). With this, we've hit rock bottom in the Johannine narrative. All that is left is for Jesus to make his way to Golgotha, "The Place of a Skull," to give his life for the sins of the world.

CRUCIFIXION, DEATH, AND
BURIAL (19:16B-42)

The remainder of the chapter divides into the narrative of the crucifixion (19:16b–27), Jesus' actual death (19:28–37), and his burial (19:38–42):

FIG. 26: THREE-PART STRUCTURE OF JOHN 19:16B-42

19:16b–27	Jesus' Crucifixion
19:28–37	Jesus' Death
19:38–42	Jesus' Burial

John records the proceedings in terse and somber language. Jesus bore his own cross (no mention of Simon of Cyrene; cf. Matt 27:32; Mark 15:21; Luke 23:26), was crucified between two others (no mention of the thief on the cross; cf. Luke 23:39–43), and was identified by a trilingual inscription on the cross—in Aramaic (or Hebrew), Latin, and Greek—as "Jesus of Nazareth, the King of the Jews" (John 19:19). All four Gospels include a version of this inscription, and their renderings contain subtle differences, which are not indicative of contradiction but rather of slight legitimate variation. Compare how the inscription reads in each of the four Gospels:

FIG. 27: THE INSCRIPTION ON THE CROSS

Matt 27:37	"This is Jesus, the King of the Jews"
Mark 15:26	"The King of the Jews"
Luke 23:38	"This is the King of the Jews"
John 19:19	"Jesus of Nazareth, the King of the Jews"

We see that none of the versions is exactly the same, though all recount the essence of the "charge" against Jesus: that he claimed—at least in Pilate's estimation—to be "the king of the Jews." All four Gospels include the verbatim phrase "the king of the Jews." Mark's version is the most concise: "The King of the Jews"; Luke's is slightly expanded: "*This is* the King of the Jews"; Matthew's is slightly more expanded: "This is *Jesus*, the King of the Jews"; and John's version, finally, is the most expansive of all: "Jesus *of Nazareth*, the King of the Jews." What a fascinating case study in the interrelationship among the four biblical Gospels! In Latin, the inscription likely read as follows (it is often abbreviated with the four initial letters "INRI"):

IESVS NAZARENVS REX IVDÆORVM
("Jesus of Nazareth, king of the Jews")

In other details surrounding the crucifixion, Jesus' seamless garment is kept in one piece in fulfillment of Scripture (19:23–24; cf. Ps 22:18); and he entrusts "the disciple whom he loved" (the apostle John) with the care of his mother (John 19:25–27), perhaps at least in part because none of his brothers are believers at this point. Jesus is given a sponge full of sour wine to quench his thirst, again in fulfillment of Scripture (19:28–29; cf. Ps 69:21); he then cries "It is finished" (Grk. *tetelestai* or its Aramaic or Hebrew equivalent) and breathes his last (John 19:30). Following Jesus' death, the soldiers do not break his legs but one of them does pierce his side, again in fulfillment of Scripture (19:32–37; cf. Ps 34:20; Zech 12:10).[6]

These details—the piercing of Jesus' side and the burial that follows—prove that Jesus truly died. If Jesus did not die, we are not actually saved. This is why the historical veracity of Jesus' real human death is vitally important: "He who saw it has borne witness—his testimony is true, and he knows that he is telling the truth—that you also may believe" (19:35). You and I can take God at his word and believe on the basis of reliable eyewitness testimony. And not only the Beloved Disciple and the women at the cross, but also the Roman soldiers and those who buried Jesus could attest that Jesus was really dead. While we may look at Jesus' death as a tragedy and wish he

---

6. See Andreas J. Köstenberger, "John," in *Commentary on the New Testament Use of the Old Testament*, ed. G. K. Beale and D. A. Carson (Grand Rapids: Baker, 2007), 415–512.

didn't have to die, the fact is that Jesus had to die, for there was no other way for us to be saved. If God had known any other way to provide salvation, he would not have sent his one and only Son to die. No earthly father would ever do that—how much less our heavenly Father![7] And yet, as John tells his readers, "For God so loved the world, that he gave his only Son, that whoever believes in him should not perish but have eternal life" (3:16).

The story of Jesus' burial is recorded in all four Gospels (19:38–42; cf. Matt 27:57–61; Mark 15:42–47; Luke 23:50–55). Joseph of Arimathea and Nicodemus, two members of the Jewish Sanhedrin, ask Pilate for permission to bury Jesus' body. (Note that only John mentions Nicodemus; the other Gospels focus on Joseph of Arimathea, in whose tomb Jesus was buried.) They rather hurriedly lay him in a new garden tomb. Then the sun sets, and Sabbath begins. There is silence, for on the Sabbath, no work must be done.

THE EMPTY TOMB AND THE RISEN JESUS (JOHN 20–21)

The last two chapters of John's Gospel are framed by stories featuring Peter and the Beloved Disciple side by side. At the beginning of John 20, after Mary Magdalene tells these two disciples that Jesus' body has gone missing, they run to the tomb and find it empty (20:3–10). At the end of John 21, Jesus gives Peter and the Beloved Disciple their marching orders (21:15–23).

In between these two framing stories, John records the moving encounter between the risen Jesus and Mary Magdalene (20:11–18)—the first to see Jesus alive after the resurrection—as well as three separate appearances by the risen Jesus to his disciples (cf. 21:14):

---

7. For one among many of Jesus' attestations to God's goodness, see Matthew 7:11 // Luke 11:13. Contra those detractors today who mischaracterize and disparage the notion of Jesus' substitutionary atonement as "cosmic child abuse." See, e.g., Steve Chalke, *The Lost Message of Jesus* (Grand Rapids: Zondervan, 2004).

FIG. 28: JESUS' POST-RESURRECTION APPEARANCES
IN JOHN'S GOSPEL

Passage	Appearance
20:19–23	To the eleven without Thomas
20:24–29	To the eleven with Thomas
21:1–14	To the seven who had gone fishing: Peter, Thomas, Nathanael, the sons of Zebedee,[8] and two others

The first appearance embeds Jesus' commission: "As the Father sent me, even so I am sending you. ... Receive the Holy Spirit" (20:21–22). The second one features doubting Thomas' remarkable confession of Jesus as his Lord and God (20:28); and the third centers on the miraculous catch of 153 fish (21:11).

The Gospel closes with the author's signature, affirming, "This is the disciple [the Beloved Disciple, cf. 21:20] who is bearing witness about these things, and who has written these things, and we know that his testimony is true" (21:24). The concluding verses also contain a reference to the abundance of available material about Jesus and an unusual first-person reference, "I suppose."

CONCLUSION

With this, our remarkable, eventful, and hopefully enlightening journey through John's Gospel has come to an end. We have seen Jesus perform seven startling messianic signs proving that he is the Christ and Son of God. We have seen him instruct his new messianic community—the twelve apostles—with regard to the coming Holy Spirit and commission them to serve as his representatives. We have heard him give his followers a "new commandment" to love each other as Jesus loved them, and we have watched him pray for the believing community's unity to undergird their mission to the world.

---

8. On the apparent "difficulty" of John, the author, referring to himself in the third person as one of "the sons of Zebedee," see my response to Richard Bauckham, chapter 1, note 14.

In our journey through the Gospel, we've been privileged to sit at the feet of the longest surviving apostle, who, according to early church tradition, in his old age wrote a complementary account of the story of Jesus based on his own eyewitness recollection. While the earlier Synoptic Gospels provided invaluable information about the life, death, burial, and resurrection of Jesus, it is John who marks the canonical capstone of the fourfold gospel in our New Testament. Fortunately, he has not left us in the dark about his purpose for writing his Gospel. Instead, he has stated explicitly that while Jesus performed many other startling signs, "these are written so that you may believe that Jesus is the Christ, the Son of God, and that by believing you may have life in his name" (20:30–31). May it be so, for his greater glory and our eternal good.

FOR FURTHER STUDY

Harris, Murray J. *John*. Exegetical Guide to the Greek New Testament. Nashville: B&H Academic, 2015.

A thorough grammatical and syntactical analysis of the Greek text of John's Gospel by a world-renowned expert in New Testament Greek.

Keener, Craig S. "John." *Zondervan Illustrated Bible Backgrounds Commentary*, vol. 2A. Edited by Clinton E. Arnold. Grand Rapids: Zondervan, 2019.

A popular-level resource on relevant background information for the study of John's Gospel.

Köstenberger, Andreas J., L. Scott Kellum, and Charles L. Quarles. *The Cradle, the Cross, and the Crown: An Introduction to the New Testament*. 2nd ed. Nashville: B&H Academic, 2016.

Covers all the relevant introductory matters related to John's Gospel.

Köstenberger, Andreas J., and Alexander E. Stewart. *The First Days of Jesus: The Story of the Incarnation*. Wheaton: Crossway, 2015.

A detailed study of the events surrounding Jesus' birth in Matthew and Luke's birth narratives; also includes a study of John's prologue.

Köstenberger, Andreas J., and Justin Taylor. *The Final Days of Jesus: The Most Important Week of the Most Important Person Who Ever Lived.* Wheaton: Crossway, 2014.

A detailed study of the events surrounding Jesus' death in all four Gospels.

Köstenberger, Andreas J. *Encountering John: The Gospel in Historical, Literary, and Theological Perspective.* Encountering Biblical Studies. 2nd ed. Grand Rapids: Baker, 2013.

An introductory textbook tracing the Johannine narrative; also includes study aids.

———. *The Jesus of the Gospels: An Introduction.* Grand Rapids: Kregel, 2020.

An introductory-level text tracing the narratives of all four Gospels: Matthew, Mark, Luke, and John, with an introductory chapter on the history of historical Jesus research.

———. "John." Pages 415–512 in *Commentary on the New Testament Use of the Old Testament.* Edited by G. K. Beale and D. A. Carson. Grand Rapids: Baker, 2007.

An in-depth study of John's use of the Old Testament, with a focus on explicit quotations.

———. *A Theology of John's Gospel and Letters: The Word, the Christ, the Son of God.* Biblical Theology of the New Testament. Grand Rapids: Zondervan, 2009.

A thorough treatment of major themes in John's Gospel and letters.

Ridderbos, Herman N. *The Gospel according to John: A Theological Commentary.* Translated by John Vriend. Grand Rapids: Eerdmans, 1992; reprint, 2018.

A classic commentary by a seasoned commentator excelling in theological synthesis.

DISCUSSION
QUESTIONS

INTRODUCTION

+ Have you ever asked God for a sign? If so, did he give you one?

+ Have you ever wished God revealed himself to you more clearly?

+ Do you think there is sufficient evidence to believe in God/Jesus?

PART 1

1. AUTHORSHIP AND JOHN'S PROLOGUE

+ Does it matter who wrote a given piece of literature? Why or why not?

+ What are the most compelling arguments for authorship of John's Gospel by the apostle John?

+ How does John's prologue function like a foyer or overture to the Gospel?

2. THE CANA CYCLE, PART 1:
THE CANA WEDDING AND THE TEMPLE CLEARING (JOHN 2)

+ How is John's Gospel similar or different than the other Gospels?

+ Why are signs so significant in John's Gospel? What is their function?

+ What qualifies the temple clearing as a sign?

3. THE CANA CYCLE, PART 2:
JESUS' CONVERSATIONS WITH NICODEMUS AND
THE SAMARITAN WOMAN (JOHN 3–4)

+ What is the function of John 2:23–25 in relation to what precedes and what follows?

+ Why is the new birth essential rather than merely optional?

+ What is John's purpose in contrasting Nicodemus and the Samaritan woman?

PART 2

4. THE FESTIVAL CYCLE, PART 1:
THE HEALING OF THE LAME MAN (JOHN 5)

+ How did John select the signs he features in his Gospel?

+ What makes John 5–10 a literary unit and why is "Festival Cycle" a fitting title?

+ How is the Festival Cycle similar or different from the Cana Cycle?

5. THE FESTIVAL CYCLE, PART 2:
THE FEEDING OF THE FIVE THOUSAND (JOHN 6)

+ What is meant by "Johannine transposition" of Synoptic material and what are examples?

+ What is the spiritual significance of the feeding of the 5,000 according to John?

+ In what ways does Jesus in John's Gospel use physical as illustrations of spiritual realities?

6. THE FESTIVAL CYCLE, PART 3:
THE HEALING OF THE MAN BORN BLIND (JOHN 9)

+ In what ways does the man born blind in chapter 9 contrast with the lame man in chapter 5?

+ In what ways does the healing of the blind man serve as a real-life parable in John's Gospel?

+ How is the spiritual principle of reversal at work in chapter 9?

PART 3

7. CONCLUSION TO THE BOOK OF SIGNS:
THE RAISING OF LAZARUS (JOHN 11)

+ In what ways does the raising of Lazarus serve as the climactic sign in John's Gospel?

+ How does the "Lazarus Cycle" in chapters 11–12 serve as a bridge to what follows?

+ How does Martha serve as a foil for John's eschatology?

8. JESUS' PREPARATION OF HIS NEW MESSIANIC COMMUNITY: THE FAREWELL DISCOURSE (JOHN 13–17)

+ What does Jesus do to prepare his followers for his imminent departure?

+ How is it better for the disciples that Jesus goes back to the Father?

+ In what ways does this unit apply uniquely to Jesus' disciples and how is it relevant for us?

9. THE JOHANNINE PASSION NARRATIVE AND EPILOGUE (JOHN 18–21)

+ In what ways is John's passion narrative similar or different from the other Gospels?

+ How does Jesus' trial before Pilate reveal the real reason why he is crucified?

+ How does Jesus' cry at the cross, "It is finished!," tie in with his identity and mission?

SUBJECT INDEX

AUTHOR INDEX

SCRIPTURE INDEX

Old Testament

Ancient Sources